THE WOUNDED WOMAN

THE WOUNDED WOMAN

Healing the Father-Daughter Relationship

Linda Schierse Leonard

SWALLOW PRESS
Athens, Ohio • Chicago

Swallow Press Books
are published by
Ohio University Press
Athens, Ohio 45701

Second printing, 1983
Third printing, 1985

Library of Congress Cataloging in Publication Data

Leonard, Linda Schierse.
 The wounded woman.

 Includes bibliographical references and index.
 1. Women—Psychology. 2. Fathers and daughters.
3. Femininity (Psychology) I. Title.
HQ1206.L43   616.89   82-6289
ISBN 0-8040-0397-1   AACR2
ISBS 0-8040-0398-X (pbk.)

HQ
1206
. L43
1982

For my Father

CONTENTS

ACKNOWLEDGMENTS

So many people have helped me over the six years of writing this book—clients, students, colleagues, friends— and I wish to thank all of these women and men who shared with me their experiences and understanding of the father-daughter relationship.

Special thanks go to the C.G. Jung Institute of San Francisco for their scholarship grants which financed some of the clerical work for this book; to the editorial staff of *Psychological Perspectives* which originally published four articles that have been incorporated in the book, and especially to William Walcott, Russell Lockhart and Al Kreinheder for their support and editorial suggestions; to Donna Ippolito of Swallow Press whose suggestions were of immeasurable importance in the final revisioning of the text; to Elaine E. Stanton for the artistic image for the cover; to Mary Ann Mattoon who first invited me to lecture publicly on the father-daughter wound and later read the manuscript and gave suggestions; to my writing group, John Beebe, Neill Russack, and Karen Signell who listened to some of the chapters in their original form and gave me new perspectives and constructive criticism; to Peer Hultberg, John Beebe, and Kirsten Rasmussen who read the manuscript as a whole and offered valuable suggestions; to my class at the California School of Professional Psychology, Berkeley, for sharing their fantasies about fathering and feminity; to Hilde Binswanger who first inspired me to write on the father-daughter wound; to Jane and Jo Wheelwright, Janine and Steve Hunter, and Gloria Gregg who gave me emotional support and suggestions during critical phases of the writing process; and especially to my mother, Virginia Schierse, who shared with me her experience and memories of my father.

Grateful acknowledgement is made to the following for permission to reprint material copyrighted or controlled by them:

"A Sword" by Karin Boye, reprinted from *The Other Voice*, copyright 1976 by W.W. Norton and Co., by permission of Albert Bonniers Förlag AB.

"What is Sorrow For?" by Robert Bly, by permission of Robert Bly.

"Why Mira Can't Go Back to her Old House," Mirabai, version by Robert Bly, reprinted by permission of Robert Bly and Sierra Club Books, from *News of the Universe*, copyright 1980 by Robert Bly.

"The Father of My Country," by Diane Wakoski, reprinted from *Inside the Blood Factory*, copyright 1968 by Diane Wakoski with permission by Doubleday Co. & Inc.

"Daddy" by Sylvia Plath, reprinted from *Ariel*, copyright 1965 by Ted Hughes, by permission of Harper & Row Publishers.

Selections from "Duino Elegies" and "Letters to a Young Poet" by Rainer Maria Rilke, copyrights 1939 and 1934 by W.W. Norton & Co., Inc. with permission of W.W. Norton and Co., Inc.

"Apotheosis" by Dawn Brett with permission by Dawn Brett.

A WOUNDED DAUGHTER

When I was a little girl I loved my father very much. He was warm and loving and was my favorite playmate. He taught me to play baseball, and he taught me mathematics. When I was seven, every Saturday he took me to the library and charmed the librarian into allowing me to check out fourteen books a week, twice their usual allotment. Because my father hadn't had a chance to finish high school, and because he valued learning so much, he communicated that value to me, and along with my grandmother, he spent hours and hours with me, helping me study and learn and improve my vocabulary, playing quiz games with me, and so on. In winter he took me sledding, and I discovered the magical brilliance of snow in the night and the excitement of the fast ride to the bottom of the hill. He also took me to the horse races where I experienced the thrills of racing and gambling. My father loved animals and so they became my friends too. And when we went on walks together, we always met new people because my father was so friendly and outgoing. I was my father's daughter, and he was so proud of me that I always had a sparkling, glowing smile. My mother was very special to him, too. Every weekend he took us out to dinner at different ethnic restaurants in the city where we lived, and then my father would often take my mother dancing until late in the night. Though we didn't have much money, life seemed to be a great adventure; there were always so many new and interesting things to see and do.

But then, somewhere, somehow, all of this started to change. My father began staying out late at night, and when he returned, I'd often be awakened by his angry shouting. At first this happened only occasionally, but soon it became once a week, then twice, and finally almost every night. In the beginning I was confused and wondered why my mother was nagging my father so much on Sunday mornings. I felt so sorry for him. But by the time I was nine years old, it became quite clear. My father was the neighborhood drunk! He couldn't hold a job, and I was now terribly ashamed of him. A photo was taken of me at the time, and the contrast between that picture and my former glowing self was remarkable. Now I looked like a forlorn waif. No longer smile and sparkling eyes, now only downcast eyes and drooping mouth. For the next several years my feelings about my father were very confused. I loved him. I suffered for him. I was ashamed of him. I wasn't able to understand how he could be so wonderful one moment and so terrible the next.

One evening stands out vividly in my memory. My father often came home late at night when he was drunk and threatened to hurt my grandmother (his mother-in-law). My mother and I often had to call the police to get him out of the house. Usually I was the one to make the call. Sometimes if my father was so violent that I couldn't get to the phone, in my fright I would run out on the porch screaming for help. On one of these especially violent nights the police arrived to find me sobbing and huddled in the corner. One policeman turned to my father and said, "How can you do this to your daughter?" The memory of this stranger's concern and his question to my father echoed in my mind for many years. It may even be that at that very moment, somewhere deep in my psyche, the seed to write this book was planted.

As I approached adolescence, my confused feelings towards my father congealed into hatred. No longer did I love him, or even pity him. Repulsed by his behavior, I hated him intensely. I lied about him to my teachers and friends, and it was impossible to invite anyone to my house. No one except our immediate neighbors knew my father was a drunk. And no one else, I pledged, would ever know—if I could help it. I disidentified with him completely, trying to become his opposite in every way I could conceive.

To protect myself, I led a double life. At school I was a hard-working, serious, straight-A student. Though I was the "teacher's pet," I also got along well with my fellow students by being pleasing and cheery, shy and adaptive. On the outside I was sweet and serious; but inside was the terrible confusion—the angry hatred of my father, the infinite shame that I was his daughter, and the fear that someone would find out who I really was. The only clues that something might be wrong were a nervous facial tic I developed at age fourteen and the fact that, unlike other girls, I didn't date. But since I had skipped a year in school and was smaller and younger than the rest, this was accepted. At school my hard work and pleasing personality brought me some comfort and meaning. But at home, life was a waking nightmare. I never knew when I'd be awakened from a deep sleep by that crazy man who was my father. I always feared the night he might come home with a gun and shoot us all.

As I grew older, I determined to escape. To stay at home, I knew, would be my demise. To protect myself from the frightening chaos of my home—from the violent and parasitic dependency of my father, and from the emotional demands my mother made on me to fill that gap her husband couldn't—I resorted to the worlds of intellect and logical thinking as a defense. This gave me the much needed distance from my mother as well, for I realized that to fulfill her desire to keep me with her in that situation would keep me forever in the prison of the past. I was trying to break my identity with both mother and father and, ultimately, from the realm of all that I could not control.

For many years, my retreat into a distant intellectual attitude served me well. I left home and worked as a newspaper reporter on a small daily newspaper in Colorado. Then I studied philosophy to develop my mind and to delve more deeply into the questions about the meaning of life. About this time I also married a man of the intellect, someone as different from my father as I could find. My husband encouraged me to continue my studies toward a Ph.D., and so my life became one of the intellect, too.

During this period my father's drinking grew progressively worse. But for my twenty-first birthday he decided to give me an opal ring, my birthstone. Somehow, although he did not work and drank up every bit of money he could get, he managed to save twenty-five dollars for that ring. The first present he had given me in many years, the ring was beautiful, sparkling with magical lights as opals do. But I couldn't wear it. The few times I came home to visit during the rest of my father's lifetime, he always asked about the ring, and I gave evasive replies. Though I felt very guilty, I simply could not bear to put on that ring. Only many years later, after his death and about the time I started writing this book, could I wear the opal birth ring. And now I wear it constantly, hoping to bridge that terrible void between my father and myself.

During my marriage, my own repressed unconscious side broke out—mysteriously and uncontrollably in the form of anxiety attacks and depression. To understand these experiences, I turned to the existentialist philosophers, Heidegger and Kierkegaard, to novelists like Dostoyevsky, Hesse, Kafka, and Kazantzakis, to poets like Rilke and Hölderlin, and finally to the psychology of C.G. Jung. Still in my professional defense system, and under the guise of deciding to become a psychotherapist myself, I went to Zürich and began a Jungian analysis. Suddenly my repressed Dionysian side emerged. My initial dream, the first dream I had after beginning analysis, was a terrible nightmare that woke me up in the middle of the night. In it, Zorba the Greek was hanging by his neck from the rafter of a ship that was on land. But he was not dead! He shouted for me to get him down, and while I fumbled about, he freed himself with tremendous effort. Then he embraced me.

Though this dream was deeply disturbing, Zorba also symbolized for me a zest for life—a carefree and playful Dionysian relationship to the world. But his world was also associated with my father, and I had seen how destructive and degenerate the journey into the irrational had been for him. Since I had consciously denied this irrational side of myself by disassociating from my father, Zorba's realm at first appeared to be chaotic, frightening, and primitive. Jung has described the way into the unconscious as a "night sea journey," a voyage of death and dismemberment, a time of terror and trembling before the awesome unknown. And this was my experience. To enter my father's world took courage, though I cannot take credit for this leap into the abyss. It forced itself on me as surely as though a silent figure had stepped behind me and pushed me over the edge of a precipice where I had been standing. There in the depths I was confronted with my own irrationality, with my own drunkenness and anger. I was just like my father after all! And many times I behaved just as he had. I became drunk at parties and a wild, seductive side of me emerged.

Face to face with the irrational realm, feeling torn to pieces like the mythical Dionysius, I began to live out my torturous dark side. My appearance changed, too, as I let my professional pixie short hair grow into a long-haired hippie style. On the walls of my apartment hung the colorful but grotesque and frightening pictures of the German expressionists. When I travelled, I sought out cheap hotel rooms in the dangerous quarters of foreign cities. Just as I had previously avoided my father's world, now I plunged head-long into it. And now I also experienced the guilt and shame that before had seemed to belong only to my father. Crazy and compulsive as all this seemed, somehow I knew there was a treasure to be found in this behavior. At one point during this chaotic period I had the following dream:

The entry to my father's house was a small shabby cellar door. Inside, I shivered as I saw the paper hang in greying clumps

xv

from the wall. Black shiny cockroaches scurried along the cracked floor and up the legs of a chipped brown table, the only piece of furniture in the bare room. The place was no bigger than a cubicle, and I wondered how anyone, even my father, could live here. Suddenly fear flooded my heart, and I sought desperately for an escape. But the door through which I had entered seemed to have disappeared in the dim light. Scarcely able to breathe, my eyes frantically roamed the room and finally caught sight of a narrow passageway, opposite to where I had entered. Eager to leave this distasteful and frightening room, I hurried through the dark passage. As I came to the end my eyes were at first blinded by the light. But then I entered into the most magnificent courtyard I had ever seen. Flowers, fountains, and marble statues of marvelous forms shone out before my eyes. Square in shape, the courtyard was really the center of an Oriental palatial temple, with four Tibetan turrets towering above each corner. Only then did I realize that all this belonged to my father too. In fear and trembling, awe and wonder, in bewilderment, I awoke from the dream.

There was indeed a passageway from the dirty, roach-infested cellar of my father's house to the shining, magnificent Tibetan temple—if only I could find it.

Although many times during this crazy and compulsive period I fell into chaos, luckily I managed somehow to function in the everyday world. But, the awareness of another, more powerful, reality was gradually entering my consciousness. Along with the devastating times were some mystical and wonderful experiences of nature. The realms of art, music, poetry, and fairy tales, the world of imagination and creativity, gradually opened up for me. From shy intellectual introvert, I became more spontaneous and able to express more warmth and feeling. Gradually I became more assertive, too, not needing to hide who I really was.

In the midst of this time two traumatic events happened to my family. My father fell asleep while drinking and smoking, and a fire began, which burned the whole house down to a blackened shell. My grandmother, trapped in an upstairs bedroom, was killed in the fire. Though my father had tried to save her, it was too late, and he was hospitalized with serious burns. How he must have suffered the guilt of this and a lifetime of self-destructive experiences! Yet, he would not or could not talk about it. Perhaps the deterioration from a lifetime of drinking was too great. Finally, two years later, he died.

My father's death was a great shock, affecting me deeply. Now it was too late to talk to him, too late ever to tell him how awful I felt for having rejected him, and how, finally, I felt some compassion for his life of suffering. Our unresolved relationship was an open wound in my psyche.

Shortly after his death, on my thirty-eighth birthday, I put on the opal ring. And then I began writing this book. Whether it might actually be published was not an issue for me. I knew then that for me to write about the father-daughter wound was imperative. Perhaps the act of writing could bring my father and me closer together. Closeness had been impossible on the outer level, but perhaps on the inner level, through this writing, I could redeem my "inner father."

Writing has been a long and difficult process for me. When I write I have no idea beforehand what I will say. I have no planned outline and I simply must wait and trust that something will come. Writing has required a commitment and an act of faith that something will appear from the depths of my psyche that I can name, that I can express, however momentarily, in words. At the same time I know that whatever I write, although it may illumine the father-daughter wound, it will also cast its shadow. There will always be a darkened spot, a side which my limited finitude cannot capture. I have had to accept this mixture of limitation and possibility, this paradox which was my father's nemesis. In the process, I have often become angry; I have often cried as well. My rage and my tears are behind every page, no matter how serene the final result may seem.

When I started writing this book, at first I saw mainly the negative patterns. I was aware of my father's legacy—his self-destruction through alcohol and how that had affected me. Although I knew there was a positive side—both to my father and his effect on me—in the early stages of writing this book I could not find it. The last chapter of my book, "Redeeming the Father," remained unwritten. Beginning with a theoretical point of view helped me gain some perspective on my conflicts. Through describing the various patterns and the underlying archetypal bases, I could better understand how these patterns worked in my life and the lives of my female clients. It was only when I started writing my personal story that my positive feelings about my father fully emerged. I realized the promise of magic he had given me when I was a little girl, the promise that later appeared in my dream of Zorba, of the Tibetan temple, and in the opal ring. My father had the promise of magical flight. But he was like the mythical Icarus who, not knowing his limits, flew so close to the sun that its heat melted the wax which held his wings and thus he plunged to his death in the sea. Similarly, my father drowned his magic in alcohol. He gave me his magic, and this was the positive part of his legacy. But as I saw him change, I saw the magic melt into degeneration. In reaction I had first denied that magical promise by trying to control everything. And then, when the controls cracked, I identified with my father's self-destructive side. My alternatives seemed to be either sterile control or Dionysian dissolution. Recognizing these two opposing extremes in myself led me to analyze the psychological patterns that I call the eternal girl (the *puella aeterna*) and the armored Amazon. Yet the resolution, the redemption, lay in the images of Zorba, the Tibetan temple, and the opal ring my father gave me. My way back to the magic of my father was to allow these images to live in myself.

This is my personal tale of a daughter's wound. But in my work as a therapist, I have discovered that many other women suffer from a wounded relationship with their fathers, although the details may differ and the wound may hurt in myriad ways. From many of my female clients I heard my own story—the alcoholic father, the resulting mistrust of men, the problems of shame, guilt, and lack of confidence. From others I learned that fathers who were strict and authoritarian might give their daughters stability, structure, and discipline, but often gave them little in the way of love, emotional support, and valuation of the feminine. Still others had fathers who wished for boys and made their daughters (usually the first-born) into sons by expecting them to accomplish what the fathers had failed to realize in their own lives. And then there were daughters whose fathers loved them too much, so that the daughters became a substitute for the lover that was missing. These women were usually so bound by their father's love that they did not feel free to love other men and thus were not able to grow up into mature womanhood. I have heard the stories of women whose fathers have committed suicide and how they themselves then had to struggle with the legacy of the death-wish and self-destruction. Women whose fathers died early have their wounds of loss and abandonment. And women whose fathers were sick often were made to feel guilty for their sickness. There are daughters whose fathers brutalized them with beatings or via sexual advances. And there are daughters whose fathers did not stand up to powerful mothers, thus allowing the mother to dominate the daughters' lives.

The list of injuries could go on and on. But there is a danger here—to blame the father for these wounds. And this would be to overlook another factor—these fathers themselves have been wounded, both in relation to their own feminine side and their own masculinity. The healing for women is not to be found in the quicksand of blame. The attitude of blame might lock us forever into the roles of passive prisoners, victims who have not assumed responsibility for our own lives. I believe it is important for such a wounded woman to understand her father's failed promise and how his lack of fatherhood has affected her life. Daughters need rapprochement with their fathers in order to develop a positive father image within themselves—one a woman can draw upon for strength and guidance and which enables her to appreciate the positive side of masculinity in both the inner and outer worlds. They need to find the hidden pearl, the treasure the father can offer. If the relationship with the father has been impaired, it is important for the woman to understand the wound, to appreciate what has been lacking so that it can be developed within. But once the injury is understood, that very wound needs to be accepted, for through acceptance of the wound comes healing and compassion—for the daughter, for the father, and for their relationship.

I.

THE WOUNDING

my father was not in the telephone book
in my city;
my father was not sleeping with my mother
at home;
my father did not care if I studied the
piano;
my father did not care what
I did;
and I thought my father was handsome and I loved him and I
    wondered
why
he left me alone so much,
so many years
in fact, but
my father
made me what I am
a lonely woman
without a purpose, just as I was
a lonely child
without any father. I walked with words, words, and names,
names. Father was not
one of my words.
Father was not
one of my names.

Diane Wakoski
"The Father of My Country"

CHAPTER ONE

THE FATHER-DAUGHTER WOUND

Now all the plagues that in the pendulous air
Hang fated o'er men's faults light on thy
daughters!
                                    Shakespeare

Every week wounded women come into my office suffering from a poor self-image, from the inability to form lasting relationships, or from a lack of confidence in their ability to work and function in the world. On the surface these women often appear quite successful—confident businesswomen, contented housewives, carefree students, swinging divorcees. But underneath the veneer of success or contentment is the injured self, the hidden despair, the feelings of loneliness and isolation, the fear of abandonment and rejection, the tears and the rage.

For many of these women, the root of their injury stems from a damaged relation with the father. They may have been wounded by a bad relation to their personal father, or wounded by the patriarchal society which itself functions like a poor father, culturally devaluing the worth of women. In either case, their self-image, their feminine identity, their relation to masculinity, and their functioning in the world is

3

frequently damaged. I would like to take the example of four women, each with a different relation to her father, each with a different lifestyle. What they have in common is inadequate fathering and a resulting way of life that obstructed their ability to form relationships and their capacity to work and to live creatively.

Chris was a successful businesswoman in her late thirties. The oldest of three daughters, she had been a hard-working, straight-A student in school. Upon graduation from college, she found a good job with a thriving company. She put so much effort into her work that by the time she was thirty Chris had risen to a top managerial position. About that time she began to experience tension headaches, insomnia, and complained of continual exhaustion. Like Atlas, she seemed to carry the weight of the world on her shoulders, and soon she became despondent and depressed. She had a series of affairs with married men whom she met in different professional contexts, but she could not seem to find a meaningful relationship. And Chris was beginning to long for a baby. She began to feel hopeless about the future, for her life had come to be merely a continual series of work obligations with no relief in sight. In her dreams were images of children who were either injured or dying. By the time Chris came into therapy, she felt trapped by a compulsion to be perfect in her work and by an inability to let go and enjoy life. She remembered her childhood as unhappy. Her parents had wanted a son, not a daughter, and her father especially expected great things from his children. If they were not the first in their class, the children soon learned they would receive disapproval from their father. To please her father, Chris had worked hard. Instead of playing with her friends, she studied and eventually went into her father's profession. Since Chris was the oldest, her father seemed to expect more of her. And when she did well, he rewarded her by taking her to his office and spending time with her there. When she reached adolescence, he was very strict, seldom allowing her to date and criticizing her few boyfriends. Her mother accepted the father's authority, completely seconding all his decisions.

In reality, Chris was living her father's life and not her own. Though she had rebelled against some of her father's values by having sexual affairs and smoking pot, in essentials she was still trying to live up to his ideal of hard work and achievement. In effect, she was still living the life her father's "son" might have led. Realizing this in the course of therapy, Chris was gradually able to let go of her compulsive perfectionism. She began to explore her own interests and started writing short stories, an activity which her father criticized as "impractical" and "indulgent." She began to meet new people, and although she still had to struggle with her tendency to be perfectionistic, she began to feel energetic and hopeful about life. For Chris to differentiate herself from her father's expectations is an ongoing process, but the more she does so, the more her own natural path continues to emerge.

A different pattern resulting from an impaired relation to the father is illustrated by the case of Barbara. When I first met her, Barbara was a student who wanted to enter graduate school. She was in her late twenties, twice divorced, with a string of abortions, a history of drug abuse, a weight problem, and a poor relation to money. Although bright and talented, her ability to work and discipline herself to study was undeveloped. Every semester, instead of finishing her course requirements, she asked her teachers for an "incomplete" grade. Soon her bill for analysis had run up to several hundred unpaid dollars. Feeling guilty about the debts and incompletes, she suffered a series of severe anxiety attacks.

Barbara had had no model for self-discipline or success. Her father had been away in wartime when she was a young child. Later, he moved from job to job and gambled, never able to settle down into anything permanent. Her mother was pessimistic and depressed and told Barbara that if she didn't succeed in marriage the first time, she would never succeed. With this combination—an unreliable father and a depressed, pessimistic mother—Barbara had no adult model

5

for success. Her dreams were frightening. Pathologically murderous men were trying to kill or cripple passive young girls. Sometimes she herself was the victim. With her loose and unstructured lifestyle, Barbara was repeating her father's pattern. She was also fulfilling her mother's negative projections that a woman could not succeed.

Once Barbara became aware that she was repeating her father's pattern and her mother's projection of failure, she began the slow and gradual process of separating herself from these patterns and finding her own path. First she learned to manage money, paid off her analytic fees, and even was able to save a sizeable amount for her future studies. To do this required giving up the drug that was eating up so much money. Eventually she was able to do her school work on schedule and wrote an outstanding dissertation. And, finally, she learned to control her eating patterns and lost twenty-five pounds. These achievements gave her a sense of her own power and the ability to accomplish what she wanted. In the course of this process the images of men and her father began to change. From destructive, murderous images, they changed to men who were helping the women figures in her dreams. In one dream her father gave her an expensive, elaborately embroidered robe, a tribute to the strength of her emerging feminine image.

Quite often women who have had easy-going, indulgent fathers who were not successful in the world will compensate for the father's lack by trying to succeed for him. Susan's father loved her very much. The two reveled in their relationship, which was playful, teasing, and flirtatious. The father put more energy into the relationship with his daughter than into the relationship with his wife. Susan's mother was a very ambitious woman who had expected great worldly achievements from her husband. That he was a simple man who enjoyed life so much that he was not at the top of his profession disappointed her deeply. Susan unconsciously had picked up this disapproval from her mother and compensated by becoming exacting and perfectionistic herself. Her father, who was dominated by his wife, did not actively oppose his wife's ambitious expectations for the daughter, and so Susan lived out her mother's unlived ambitions. Caught by her mother's ambitious, controlling, perfectionistic attitude, Susan lost her relationship to her relaxed, easy-going, child-like side. The resulting tension brought her neck and back strain during the day, insomnia and teeth grinding at night. No matter what she did, it was never good enough. Although Susan loved her father, she feared that men were weak and incapable. Like her mother, Susan wanted a man who was ambitious and a highly successful moneymaker, but she was attracted to fun-loving men like her father, who in the end proved to be too unreliable for a committed relationship. Just as nothing she did was good enough, neither were her lovers able to satisfy her perfectionistic standards. Now in her forties, she remained unmarried. She also attempted to control things in the areas of work and relationships, with a resulting depression and boredom. Resenting the joylessness of her life, she was taken over by a martyred attitude of hopelessness. At the same time she began to feel she couldn't meet one more commitment in her professional life, that she would collapse under all those demands. Her dreams, however, brought up some positive images that showed another approach. In one dream, after she had chosen the hardest and fastest way to get where she was going, a voice told her to slow down and take an easier path, assuring Susan she would get there in her own good time. In other dreams she found herself floating peacefully down a river.

Susan began to realize that much of her push, drive, and urge to control belonged to her mother rather than herself. She also became aware that the depression she felt when she did not succeed was much like the depression her father fell into when criticized by his wife. She also saw that in many ways she had acted the role of her father's "lover," and that this cut her off from relationships with other men. Consciously, she began to counter the inner voice that critically judged herself and others. She became more open to men and tried to know them without judging them first. Eventually she met a warm, affectionate man, but for some time she was tempted to end the relationship because he wasn't earning as much money as she thought he should. When she was able to recognize these criticisms as part of her mother's voice, Susan was able to allow the relationship to live.

In this case the mother was the more dominant figure; the father's negligence consisted of not opposing the mother's compulsive ambitions. In a way, he loved his daughter "too much" and so kept her tied to him. Susan needed to recognize this to break the tight bind to her father and to see the effects of her mother's influence.

Sometimes, as in the case of Mary, a daughter rebels against an overly authoritarian and rigid father. Her father was in the military and required military performance even from his children. Mary, whose temperament was friendly and spontaneous, rebelled against her father's authoritarian attitude. As a teenager she took LSD and ran around with a fast crowd. Although she had artistic talent, Mary let it slide and then quit college in her sophomore year. Despite her father's authoritarian and perfectionistic tendencies, he had a chronic disease which forced him to show vulnerability and weakness. Since he never admitted his vulnerability Mary experienced her father as though he were two different people—the strong, authoritarian judge, and the weak, sick man. The men in her dreams also appeared in these opposing ways. There were men with tiny phalluses who were impotent, and there were violent men trying to stab and kill her. Mary felt that the impotent men symbolized her tremendous lack of self-confidence, and that the violent, attacking men were the voice of self-depreciation. Mary's mother was much like herself, a warm, outgoing woman, but she did not oppose her husband, Since Mary had a good relationship with her mother, she first turned to an older woman for support. But in this relationship she tended to play the role of pleasing daughter, while the older woman often criticized her in an authoritarian manner similar to that of Mary's father. In the course of analysis she began to gain confidence in herself and recognized the double pattern of rebelling against the authority of the father, yet submitting to it by pleasing the older authoritarian woman. Eventually she was able to assert herself in relation to her older woman friend. Then as the threatening men and the impotent men began to disappear from her dreams, she began a relationship with an emotionally mature man whom she later married. She now had enough confidence in herself to accept the challenge of returning to her love of art and began to study a career in this field. With her new-found strength she was even able to have a meaningful talk with her father, who, in a moment of crisis due to his illness, acknowledged his vulnerability. This enabled a closer emotional relationship between father and daughter.

These are only four examples of wounded women who have suffered from injured relationships with their fathers. There are many variations on this theme. The following dream reveals the general psychological situation of a wounded woman who suffers from an impaired relation to the father.

I am a young girl trapped in a cage holding my baby. Outside is my father riding freely on a horse over green pastures. I long to reach him and try to get out of the cage, sobbing deeply. But the cage topples over. I am not sure whether my baby and I will be crushed by the cage or whether we will be free.

This dream images the separation between father and daughter and the imprisonment of the daughter and her creative potentialities. There is the longing to reach the free energy of the father. But the daughter must first get out of the cage, and this requires a risk. She and her baby may be crushed in the process, or they also may go free. While this is the dream of only one woman, I believe it portrays dramatically the way many other women have been imprisoned by a poor relation to the father, alienating them from a positive relation to fathering in themselves.

9

On the personal level, there are many ways the father-daughter wound can occur. The father may have been extremely weak and a cause of shame for his daughter; for example, a man who can't hold a job or who drinks or gambles, etc. Or he may be an "absent father," having left home by choice as does the man who "loves 'em and leaves 'em." The absence may also be due to death, war, divorce, or illness—each of which separates the father from his family. Still another way a father can wound a daughter is to indulge her so much that she has no sense of limit, values, and authority. He may even unconsciously fall in love with her and thus keep her bound to him in this way. Or he may look down upon and devalue the feminine because his own inner feminine side has been sacrificed to the ideals of macho-masculine power and authority. He may be a hard worker, successful in his profession, but passive at home and not really actively involved with his daughter, i.e., a detached father. Whatever the case may be, if the father is not there for his daughter in a committed and responsible way, encouraging the development of her intellectual, professional, and spiritual side and valuing the uniqueness of her femininity, there results an injury to the daughter's feminine spirit.

"The Feminine" is an expression that is currently being re-discovered and re-described anew by women out of their own experiences. Women have begun to realize that men have been defining femininity through their conscious and culturally conditioned expectations of women's roles and through their unconscious projections on women. In contrast to the notion of femininity defined from a cultural or biological role, my approach is to see "the feminine" symbolically as a way of being, as an inherent principle of human existence. In my experience the feminine reveals itself primarily via images and emotional responses and I draw upon these in the course of this book.[1]

The father-daughter wound is not only an event happening in the lives of individual women. It is a condition of our culture as well.[2] Whenever there is a patriarchal authoritarian attitude which devalues the feminine by reducing it to a number of roles or qualities which come, not from woman's own experience, but from an abstract view of her—there one finds the collective father overpowering the daughter, not allowing her to grow creatively from her own essence.

Whether the father-daughter wound occurs on the personal level or the cultural level, or both, it is a major issue for most women today. Some women try to avoid dealing with it by blaming their fathers and/or men in general. Others may try to avoid it by denying there is a problem and living out the traditionally accepted feminine roles. But both these routes result in giving up responsibility for their own transformation, the one via blame, the other via adaptation. I believe the real task for women's transformation these days is to discover for themselves who they are. But part of this discovery entails a dialogue with their history, with the developmental influences that have affected them personally, culturally, and spiritually.

As a daughter grows up, her emotional and spiritual growth is deeply affected by her relationship to her father. He is the first masculine figure in her life and is a prime shaper of the way she relates to the masculine side of herself and ultimately to men. Since he is "other," i.e., different from herself and her mother, he also shapes her differentness, her uniqueness and individuality. The way he relates to her femininity will affect the way she grows into womanhood. One of his roles is to lead the daughter from the protected realm of the mother and the home into the outside world, helping her to cope with the world and its conflicts. His attitude toward work and success will color his daughter's attitude. If he is confident and successful, this will be communicated to his daughter. But if he is afraid and unsuccessful, she is likely to take over this fearful attitude. Traditionally, the father also projects ideals for his daughter. He provides a model for authority, responsibility, decision-making, objectivity, order, and discipline. When she is old enough, he steps back so she may internalize these ideals and

11

actualize them in herself. If his own relation to these areas is either too rigid or too indulgent, that will affect his daughter's relation to these areas as well.[3]

Some fathers err on the side of indulgence. Because they have not established limits for themselves, because they do not feel their own inner authority and have not established a sense of inner order and discipline, they provide inadequate models for their daughters. Such men often remain "eternal boys" (the *puer aeternus*). Men who identify too strongly with this god of youth stay fixated at the adolescent stages of development.[4] They may be romantic dreamers who avoid the conflicts of practical life, unable to make commitments. Such men tend to dwell in the realm of possibilities, avoiding actuality, leading a provisional life. Quite often they are close to the springs of creativity and are sensitive searchers for spirit. But since their interior year centers around spring and summer, the depth and rebirth which comes from fall and winter is lacking. By disposition, this type of man tends to be impatient. He has not developed the quality to "hold," to bear through a difficult situation. Positively, he is often charming, romantic, and even inspiring, for he reveals spirit in the form of possibility, the creative spark, the search. But negatively considered, his tendency is not to carry anything through to completion since he avoids hard times and the down-to-earth work and struggle required to actualize the possible. Some extreme examples of these men who remain eternal boys can be found in addicts who remain forever dependent on their addiction, men who cannot work, Don Juan men who run from woman to woman, men who remain passive sons to their wives, and men who seduce their daughters by romanticizing them. A few are dazzlingly successful for a brief period, such as the movie star James Dean and the rock star Jim Morrison, only to succumb to their self-destructive tendencies, leaving a legend and even a cult behind, emphasizing the archetypal character of their fascination.

The daughters of these eternal boys grow up without an adequate model of self-discipline, limit, and authority, quite often suffering from feelings of insecurity, instability, lack of self-confidence, anxiety, frigidity, and, in general, a weak ego. Moreover, if the father was overtly weak (as in the cases of the man who doesn't work or the addict), the daughter is likely to suffer from a sense of shame. And if she was ashamed of her father, she is likely to carry this sense of shame over to herself. In such cases, she often unconsciously builds up an ideal image of man and father, and her life may become a search for this ideal father. In seeking the ideal, she is likely to be bound to a "ghostly lover," i.e., the ideal man who exists only in her imagination.[5] Hence, her relationship with men, especially in the sphere of sexuality, is likely to be disturbed. The lack of commitment she experienced with her father is likely to produce a general lack of trust in men which may extend also to the whole realm of spirit, i.e., metaphorically speaking, to "God the Father." At the deepest level, she suffers from a religious problem since, for her, spirit was not provided by the father. How, then, is she to find it? Anaïs Nin, who had such a father, has expressed it: "I have no guide. My father? I think of him as someone my own age."[6]

Other fathers err on the side of rigidity. Hard, cold, and sometimes indifferent, they enslave their daughters through a strict authoritarian attitude. These men are quite often exiled from the vitality of life, cut off from their own feminine sides and from feeling. Their emphasis tends to be on obedience, duty, and rationality. And they insist that their daughters have the same values. Obedience to the established order is the rule. Departure from society's norm is looked on with suspicion and distrust. These fathers are often domineering old men, frequently embittered, cynical, and sapped of life. Because their emphasis is on control and doing things right, frequently they are not open to the unexpected, to the expression of creativity and feelings. And they tend to treat such things with sarcasm and derision. On the positive side, their emphasis on authority and duty provides a sense of security, stability, and structure. On the negative side, it tends to squash "feminine" qualities of feeling, sensitivity, and spontaneity. Some extreme examples of fathers who function as domineering old men can be found among the old patriarchs who retain control of all the money, dominating their wives and children financially, fathers who make all the rules and require obedience, fathers who expect their daughters to achieve inordinate success in the world, fathers who demand that their daughters follow the conventional feminine roles, fathers who cannot acknowledge any sign of weakness, sickness, or even difference from themselves.

In later life the daughters of these domineering old men often find themselves cut off from an easy relation to their own feminine instincts, since their own fathers could not truly acknowledge their femininity. Since these women experienced strictness and harshness from their fathers, they are likely to be hard either on themselves or others. Even if they rebel, one often feels in that rebellion something relentless and sharp. Some daughters knuckle under to the authoritarian rule and never live their own lives. Others, though they may rebel, stay bound to their father's control, living always in reaction to him. These daughters, too, like those of the more indulgent fathers, tend to be cut off from a healthy relationship to men and to their own creative spirit.

So far, I have described two extreme tendencies that may exist in a father's relationship to his daughter. But most fathers are a mixture of the two. And even if a father has lived out his life in only one of these two extremes, he often acts out the other extreme unconsciously.[7] There are many examples of rigidly authoritarian fathers who suddenly fly into irrational, emotional outbursts which threaten all the security and order they have established, instilling a terrible fear of chaos in their daughters. Since the feeling realm is not consciously acknowledged by the father, but instead seems to overwhelm him from time to time, it seems all the more threatening to his children. Sometimes these rages have sexual overtones as well—for example, the father who physically punishes a disobedient daughter in such a way that she becomes threatened on the sexual level. So, while the father's conscious emphasis may be on duty, rationally toeing the line, in the background may be puerile moods and impulses which pop out unconsciously at unexpected moments. In the same way, indulgent fathers are likely to have in the background of their lives the sneering cynicism of the rigid judge. Such a father may suddenly turn on his daughter, criticizing her for those impulsive qualities he dislikes in himself.

Obviously, the role of the mother is another important factor in the daughter's development.[8] Since my purpose in this book is to focus on the father-daughter relationship, I do not go into the mother's influence in any breadth or depth, but only hint in that direction. Quite often one finds certain pairs in a marriage. The father who is an eternal boy often has a "mother" for a wife. In these cases, the mother often rules the home and is the disciplinarian for the family. Through her alone come the values, order, authority, and structure that is usually provided by the father. Sometimes such a mother can be more rigid than the most rigid of old men fathers. And together with that comes the force of her female emotions. When the father is weak and indulgent and the mother strong and controlling, the daughter has a double problem. Not only is the father not able to provide her with a masculine model, but he does not stand up to the mother and help the daughter differentiate herself from her mother. The daughter may remain bound and identified with the mother. In this case, she is likely to adopt unconsciously the same rigid attitudes as her mother. In addition, when the mother has to function as the father, sometimes the daughter receives neither genuine fathering nor mothering.

A contrasting pair is the rigid old man father who has a girl for a wife. In this case, both mother and daughter are dominated, and the mother in her passive dependence does not provide a model for genuine feminine independence. So the daughter is likely to repeat the pattern of feminine dependence, or, if she rebels, she does so out of a defensive reaction against paternalistic authority rather than out of her own feminine needs and values.

It is also possible for both father and mother to be eternal youths, in the fashion of Scott and Zelda Fitzgerald, and then

15

there is usually little stability, structure, or authority provided by either parent. In these cases, the commitment of both parents is often tenuous and the marriage and family may dissolve, leaving the daughter in chaos and anxiety. Or, it may be that both father and mother are rigid elders, both ruling with tight reign. And then the daughter is cut off on both sides from the sources of spontaneity and feeling.

In myself and in my female clients, I have found two opposing patterns that frequently result from a wounded relation to the father. And these two conflicting patterns frequently exist together in the psyche of a wounded woman, doing battle with each other. One pattern I call "the eternal girl" (or *puella aeterna*).[9] The other I call the "armored Amazon." Here I want only briefly to describe each pattern in broad strokes, since each is described in more detail in later chapters.

The "eternal girl," or puella, is a woman who psychologically has remained a young girl, even though chronologically she may be sixty or seventy years of age. She remains a dependent daughter, tending to accept the identity others project upon her. In doing so, she gives over to others her own strength as well as the responsibility for shaping her identity. Quite often she marries a rigidly authoritarian man and becomes the image of woman he wants. Often she looks and acts innocent, helpless, and passive. Or she may rebel, but in her rebellion remains the helpless victim caught in feelings of self-pity, depression, and inertia. In either case, she is not directing her own life.

In the dreams of such women, I have found several recurrent images. One dream theme is the loss of one's pocketbook, with all one's identity cards and money. For example, one woman dreamt that her man friend had left her, and when she tried to go home, she realized she had no money. The only means of transportation she could take was a school bus for children. Another frequent dream theme revealing a basic dependence is not to be driving one's own car, often sitting in the back seat feeling helpless and out of control while the father drives. Still another frequent image in the dreams of women who psychologically remain young girls is that of a mean old man chasing, threatening, and sometimes brutally dominating them. One young woman with whom I worked dreamt she was on a high diving board while a sadistic old man kept demanding she do increasingly more dangerous dives. Unless she stopped following his commands, she was in danger of losing her life. These dream motifs reveal the danger of losing one's own source of energy and identity (symbolized by the loss of money and pocket-book), the danger of losing direction over one's own life (symbolized by not driving the car), and the danger of not asserting oneself against unreasonable commands (following the sadistic man's orders).

Quite often the woman who remains an eternal girl has failed to identify with and integrate the qualities a positive father can help her develop: consciousness, discipline, cour-age, decision-making, self-valuation, direction. Many women in our culture today have found themselves in this position because the "cultural fathers" have not encouraged women to develop these qualities. And frequently women have actually been discouraged from this development. The result is disastrous, leaving the woman feeling weak and helpless, without resources, afraid to strike out on her own, and under the rule of old-fashioned, domineering, patriarchal princi-ples. I have seen these patterns operate in myself and in the lives of many women who remain stuck in the puella pattern of the eternal girl. It is as though the masculine side of a woman is split into two opposites: weak young boy and perverted, sadistic old man. This combination keeps a woman from developing, since in the unconscious these two male figures secretly work together. The voice of the per-verted old man says, "You cannot do it—you're just a woman." And the weak, sensitive boy gives in to those feelings of weakness which keep her from getting out of the destructive pattern. How many times must this happen to women in our culture when they give in to helpless and

17

negative feelings which say they cannot create, or that all men are rotten and will only betray them. It is then that they have lost their spirit!

The "armored Amazon" is a contrasting pattern in the lives of many women. Developmentally, I find that this pattern arises as a reaction against inadequate fathering, occurring either on the personal or cultural level. In reacting against the negligent father such women often identify on the ego level with the masculine or fathering functions themselves. Since their fathers didn't give them what they needed, they find they have to do it themselves. So they build up a strong masculine ego identity through achievement or fighting for a cause or being in control and laying down the law themselves, perhaps as a mother who rules the family as though it were a business firm. But this masculine identity is often a protective shell, an armor against the pain of abandonment or rejection by their fathers, an armor against their own softness, weakness, and vulnerability. The armor protects them positively insofar as it helps them develop professionally and enables them to have a voice in the world of affairs. But insofar as the armor shields them from their own feminine feelings and their soft side, these women tend to become alienated from their own creativity, from healthy relationships with men, and from the spontaneity and vitality of living in the moment.

In my office every day I see women who are successful in the world, accomplished in their fields, financially independent. To the outer eye they seem secure and confident, powerful and strong. But inside the safety of the therapist's office they reveal their tears, the confessions of weariness and exhaustion, the great loneliness. Many times the image of armor comes up in their dreams. One woman dreamt of a weak little man, tired of life and about to die, who was dressed in a protective coat of armor and helmet, shield and sword. Later on in the course of analysis, as she let go of the unnecessary armor, she dreamt she found a diamond treasure hidden in a pile of open oyster shells. Her emphasis now was on being in the moment and open to relationships, and she felt softer and more mellow. The shell was now open and the genuine diamond strength accessible.

In another woman's dreams, the armor theme came up in the image of heavy winter coats. In one dream, it was summer and as she left her childhood home, she realized she was carrying several heavy wooden hangers for winter coats, but the coats were gone. She felt she had lost her protection. As she left this house, two young men were behind her. They were lighthearted lads, full of fun and tricks, and she was afraid of them. So she speeded up her pace to get away from them, but they skipped lightly by and one untied her shoelace. Now she was terrified and, in trying to escape, ran into a forbidding-looking house full of paralyzed and crazy women. Needless to say, she awoke in horror. In reality this woman needed to drop the winter coat protection and learn to play with the lighthearted lads, but she was still frightened of them.

The woman dressed in Amazon armor is as cut off from her own center as is the eternal girl. In fact, in most women, these two patterns tend to exist together. In my own experience, the Amazon armor came first. But behind that was the frightened little girl who finally emerged and then flew off unable to settle here or there, unable to commit herself to a place or a person. Other women have started out as compliant, charming wives and turned into actively angry fighters. In most women, the two patterns are there alternating, sometimes from moment to moment. For example, one woman who did a lot of public speaking still felt like the fragile girl who was afraid she might faint before everyone, yet side by side within her were feelings of competency and authority as a speaker. She was amazed to find that other people, and especially men, experienced her as strong and competent when inwardly she felt shy and scared.

Why one woman initially follows the path of the eternal girl while another takes the route of the armored Amazon is for me still a big question and remains to be explored. My hunch is that a variety of factors contribute to which way a woman takes. Innate temperament and one's position and role in the family seem to be major factors. The relationship to the mother is another. Body-type, racial, and socio-economic class differences are other significant aspects. Quite often I find that the oldest daughter tends to take the Amazon route while the younger daughter becomes the eternal girl. But this is not always the case. Whether one identifies with the father or mother, and repeats or rebels against whomever is the dominant parent is another factor. In my experience these two patterns (the eternal girl and the armored Amazon) are present in most women, although one may be lived out more consciously than the other.

Both the eternal girl and the armored Amazon quite often find themselves in despair over their condition. They feel alienated from their center because they are cut off from important parts of themselves. It is as though they have a mansion for their home but are only living in a few of the rooms.

The philosopher, Søren Kierkegaard, helped me to understand in myself and in the lives of my clients the source of this alienation and despair. Kierkegaard, in *Sickness Unto Death*, analyzes despair as a disrelationship to the Self, to the source of being human.[10] For Kierkegaard there are three major forms of despair: first, despair that is unconscious; second, despair that is conscious and which manifests itself as weakness; and third, despair which is conscious and manifests itself as defiance.

In the unconscious form of despair, the person is out of relation to the Self, but is unaware of it. Such a person, according to Kierkegaard, tends to live a hedonistic life, dispersed in sensation of the moment, having no commitment to anything higher than ego-impulses. This is the stage of aestheticism and Don Juanism. Here one can see a type of existence in which people do not consciously realize they are in despair, although, as Kierkegaard points out, the compulsiveness for infinite sensation and pleasure together with intruding dark moments of boredom and anxiety reveal that all is not well.

If the person allows the dark moments of boredom and anxiety to enter fully into consciousness, then comes the awareness of despair, the realization of disrelationship to the Self, and the feeling that one is too weak to choose the Self since that demands the acceptance of one's strength to make that decision. Here the person despairs over weakness to commit to something higher than ego-impulses. I imagine that many puellas suffer intensely in the despair of weakness—wanting to be courageous and take the risk of actuality, the risk of commitment, yet somehow afraid and unable to take the leap.

But if the person penetrates more consciously into the reason for weakness, then comes awareness that the excuse of weakness was really only a way of avoiding the strength already there. What the person originally took to be weakness is now understood to be defiance, i.e., a refusal to commit! For Kierkegaard, the despair of defiance is a higher consciousness, a realization that one has the strength to choose the Self, or in Kierkegaard's terms, to make the leap of faith which requires acceptance of the uncontrollable and transcendent, but that one chooses not to do so in stark defiance against the powers which transcend reason and man's finitude. In defiance, one refuses to change! In the despair of defiance, one refuses possibility and infinitude. In the despair of weakness, one refuses actuality and finitude. To refuse one is to refuse both. The despair of weakness I see to be an aspect of the eternal girl. The despair of defiance appears to me to be an aspect of the armored Amazon. And yet in the end they are secretly the same—two poles of a split in the self.

Women who fall into the archetypal pattern of the puella, caught in the despair of weakness, need to become aware of their strength and shake off their victim identity. Women who are caught in the armored Amazon's tendency to control need to see how control can be a false strength and to value the openness to what cannot be controlled. For Kierkegaard, resolution and transformation come ultimately when despair in all stages is overcome through a leap of faith. In this leap one accepts at the same time one's weakness and one's strength, the intermixture of the finite and infinite realms in being human, and the realization that human beings must

21

move between the opposites rather than identifying with an absolute.

Therapeutically, I found in the work of the psychiatrist Carl Gustav Jung a great help in understanding this kind of situation which exists in many people's lives. Jung thought that the life of each person was a complex and mysterious whole. But the particular course of their development, coming from personal family experiences, cultural influences, and innate temperament, tended to lead a person to emphasize one part of the personality and to de-emphasize the conflicting part. Yet, that other opposing, unaccepted side was there wanting to be acknowledged and often intruded upon the consciously accepted side, affecting the person's behavior and disturbing his or her relationships. Jung thought the task of personal growth was to see the value of both sides and to try to integrate them so that they could work together in a fruitful way for the person. I find this to be important therapeutically for the wounded woman who finds herself in a conflict between these two patterns: the eternal girl and the armored Amazon. Each has its value. Each can learn from the other. And the integration of the two is a foundation for the emerging woman.

Although a woman may be wounded from an impaired relation to the father, it is possible for her to work towards healing the wound. We bear the influences of our parents, but we are not fated to remain merely the products of our parents. There is in the psyche, according to Jung, a natural healing process which moves toward balance and wholeness. In the psyche also are natural patterns of behavior which he called archetypes and which are available to serve as inner models, even when outer models are absent or unsatisfactory. A woman has within herself, for instance, all the potentialities of the father archetype, and these can often be reached if she is willing to risk coming in touch with the unconscious. So, even though the personal or cultural fathers initially may have shaped the conscious image of ourselves as women and what we can do in the world and in relation to men, there is within us as well the positive and creative aspects of the inner archetypal father which can compensate for many of the negative influences in our actual life histories. This potentiality to gain a better relationship to the father principle is one we all have within us. Dream images often reveal previously unknown sides of the father that we can experience in order to become more whole and mature. The following case illustrates this view.

One woman with whom I worked grew up under the authoritarian rule of a rigid father who did not value the feminine. Hard work and discipline, masculine occupations were what he stressed. Weakness or vulnerability of any kind was not allowed. So the daughter adopted these values and always kept very busy planning and controlling her life. She didn't allow herself to relax or to show any weakness. But this put her at an emotional distance from others and at a distance from her own heart center. She came into therapy shortly after she developed a skin disease which became more and more visible to others. It was as though her vulnerability wanted to be acknowledged. She couldn't hide it anymore, for there it was on her skin for all to see. In the initial dream she had at the start of therapy she was stranded high on the tower of a skyscraper. Up there she could see all the plan of traffic flow in the city, but she couldn't get down to the ground to do anything. At last a fun-loving man climbed up the tower and helped her down to earth, and then she ran barefoot with him, playing on the grass. This dream showed the side of the masculine that had been missing in her development since it wasn't provided by her stern and serious father. She needed to relate to an instinctual man who could play with her.

Early in the analysis she also had a dream which showed the influence of her father. In the dream she wanted to show her father her skin disease, but he refused to look at it. He refused to allow her any vulnerability and she had unconsciously adopted his attitude towards herself. This affected not only her emotional life but also her creativity. Although she had a great deal of artistic talent and creative potential, she went into one of the more rational sciences, and then never finished her studies. It was as though she was on her father's path and not her own. In the course of analysis, she began to accept her vulnerable side and allowed herself to play. The man in her first dream provided an image to accept those areas of herself. On the outer level she then met a warm, spontaneous man with whom she fell in love, opening up her vulnerable side. She started school again, this time also in an area which she loved. Shortly after this, the image of her father changed in her dreams. In one dream she was told her father had died. Then she heard a bell calling her to the other side of the river. She started to go across on a bridge, but the bridge was not quite finished and so she slid into the water to get across. The death of the father symbolized the end of his rigid reign, and now she was called to cross over to the other side of the river to a new side of herself. The bridge to that new side was already partly built, but she had to get into the water to cross all the way. For her this meant to get into the flow of life and her feelings. As she did so, the image of her father changed in her dreams, and he became more accepting. In one dream she had lost something that belonged to him and instead of rebuking her for her failure, he accepted her. In another dream her father was working for a creative rock musician and she was proud of him. It was as though the dreams and her life were dancing together, each making new movements in turn so that she was able to move into a new rhythmic way of being. Through her pursuit of self-knowledge and relating to her dreams in therapy, she was able to connect with her playful, flowing feeling side, and her femininity and creativity were released. When she experienced the compensatory energies of the father archetype within, the old wound coming from her stern, rigid, and unaccepting father began to heal.

CHAPTER TWO
SACRIFICE OF THE DAUGHTER

Your nature, princess, is indeed noble and true;
But events fester, and divinity is sick.

Euripides

The father-daughter wound is a condition of our culture and, to that extent, the plight of all men and women today. Women frequently are considered inferior to men. Men often are put down if they show feminine qualities. Implicit in the father-daughter wound is a disturbed relation between the masculine and feminine principles.[1] And this affects not only individuals but also partners, groups, and whole societies. Both men and women suffer from it. Both are confused about their own identities and roles vis-à-vis the other.

The roots of the father-daughter wound are deep and can be seen clearly in the Greek drama *Iphigenia in Aulis* by Euripides. The drama shows how a father comes to sacrifice his daughter and portrays the wound the father feels when he is driven to this end. It also reveals the limited view of the feminine in a patriarchally ruled society. Iphigenia is the oldest and the most beloved daughter of King Agamemnon. And yet, in the play, she is sacrificed, sentenced to death by her very own father, who loves her most dearly. How can this happen? How is it possible for a father to sacrifice a daughter?

At the play's beginning we find Agamemnon in deep despair, halfway to madness, because he has agreed to the sacrifice of his daughter, Iphigenia. The Hellenes had pledged war on Troy because the Trojan, Paris, had stolen Helen, most beautiful of women and the wife of Agamemnon's brother, Menelaus. But when the army went to Aulis Bay, ready to sail for battle, there was no wind. Crazed with the lust for battle, the army became impatient and Agamemnon's rule was threatened. Fearing the loss of his power and glory and the command of the army, Agamemnon consulted an oracle that said he must sacrifice his first-born daughter for the greater glory of Greece. The sacrifice was to be made to the goddess Artemis in exchange for wind to sail. In despair, Agamemnon finally agreed to the decree and sent for Iphigenia, saying that she was to be married to Achilles. But this was only a pretext to get Iphigenia to Aulis for the sacrifice. Later Agamemnon realized the madness of what he had done, but it was too late.

Angrily, Agamemnon accused Menelaus of being a dupe of beauty and of being willing to throw away his reason and honor for it. Menelaus accused Agamemnon of agreeing to the sacrifice of Iphigenia to save his own power. While the two brothers were fighting angrily, Iphigenia arrived, and Agamemnon felt powerless in the grip of fate. Even though Menelaus in a moment of sudden compassion realized he had been wrong and urged Agamemnon not to sacrifice his daughter, Agamemnon now felt compelled to go ahead with it. He was afraid that if he refused, the enraged masses would revolt, sacrificing not only Iphigenia but himself as well. And so King Agamemnon, ruled by his own service to power and to the glory of Greece, and by his fear, felt forced to kill his daughter Iphigenia.

When Iphigenia and her mother, Clytemnestra, arrived in Aulis, they were happy with the plan for Iphigenia to marry Achilles. But Iphigenia found her father strangely sad and worried. And when Agamemnon commanded Clytemnestra

26

to leave Aulis before her daughter's wedding, she thought this strange and refused. Finally she discovered the plot to sacrifice her daughter and she was outraged. Achilles, too, became angry, learning he had been duped by Agamemnon, and swore to protect Iphigenia with his life. In horrified despair, Clytemnestra confronted Agamemnon with what she had heard. At first he evaded and denied the accusation, but finally he admitted to the awful truth. Incensed, Clytemnestra charged him with more shame—that he had killed her first husband and her baby and had taken her by force. But when her own father condoned the marriage, she submitted and had become an obedient wife. Clytemnestra tried to shame Agamemnon into changing his mind. And Iphigenia pleaded with her father for her life. Both asked why Helen, who was Clytemnestra's sister and Iphigenia's aunt, should be more important than his daughter. But Agamemnon, feeling helpless before the demonic lust for power of the army, pledged his first duty to Greece and said he had no other choice.

At first Iphigenia cursed Helen; she cursed her murderous father; and she cursed the lustful army bound for Troy. But when even Achilles was helpless against the army's raging masses, she gave in. She resolved to die nobly for Greece, since all Hellas looked to her for the sailing of the fleet. Why should Achilles die for her, she asked, when "One man is of more value than a host of women."[2] And who was she, a mortal, to oppose the divine Artemis? But the Greek Chorus, speaking for the truth, replied, "Your nature, princess, is indeed noble and true; But events fester, and divinity is sick."[3] Nevertheless, Iphigenia went nobly to her death, absolving her father and telling her mother not to be angry and not to hate him.[4]

What view of the feminine is implied in this drama? Woman is regarded as man's possession! The three prominent female characters are regarded as objects owned by man. Because Menelaus regards Helen as his possession, the loss of the beautiful Helen initiates the Greeks to war on the Trojans to retrieve her. Clytemnestra, the obedient wife, is regarded by Agamemnon as his to rule. And Iphigenia is a daughter who can be sacrificed by her father. Hence, the feminine is not allowed to reveal itself from its own center, but is reduced to those forms compatible with the prevailing masculine view.

At the same time, the prevailing masculine goal is power; man's first duty is to Greece, no matter what the cost. Helen's seduction by Paris is really an opportunity for the Greeks to make war on the Trojans. As Agamemnon later realizes when it is too late, "A strange lust rages with demonic power throughout the Hellene army..."[5] And it is this power lust which ultimately demands Iphigenia's sacrifice.

This drama also shows a split within the feminine. One role is allotted to Helen who personifies beauty. Another is given to Clytemnestra, the obedient and dutiful wife and mother. These two forms of the feminine are the only roles for women that this play presents. The feminine realm is devalued by being reduced to the service of men either through beauty or obedience. The ideal of beauty reduces the woman's worth to a mere projection of men's desire and puts her in the puella position of girl-like dependence. And dutiful obedience reduces her to the status of servant to a male master. In each case she exists not in and of herself, but has her identity only in relation to man's needs. The father, King Agamemnon, supports this devaluation of the feminine when ultimately he agrees to sacrifice his daughter so that the Greeks can bring back Helen. And he expects his wife, Clytemnestra, to be ruled by his decree. His own ambition and need for power is primary, and the welfare of his daughter is only secondary.

Just as the two sisters, Helen and Clytemnestra, personify the split feminine ideals of beauty and obedience, so the two brothers, Menelaus and Agamemnon, are ruled in soul by these two opposites. Menelaus, the boyish brother, is so captivated by Helen's beauty that he is willing to sacrifice all else—a whole army of men and even his niece's life. In contrast, Agamemnon has sold his soul to serve Greece's lust for power and for his own ambition to be king even though this position isolates him and cuts him off from expressing his human fatherly feelings. Perhaps the worst wound Agamemnon suffers is to be cut off from his tears. As he confesses:

> What a man-trap of compulsive Fate I have fallen into! Some divine power, cleverer than all my cleverness has tricked and defeated me. To be low-born, I see, has its advantages: A man can weep, and tell his sorrows to the world. A king endures sorrows no less; but the demand for dignity governs our life, and we are slaves to the masses. I am ashamed to weep; and equally I am ashamed not to weep, in such a depth of grief.[6]

What is the trap that Agamemnon, the king and father, has fallen into? Spirit seems to be impotent, symbolized by the lack of wind. And as the Chorus has announced: "...events fester, and divinity is sick." Agamemnon is caught in man's willful striving for power in the name of Greece, and so his daughter is sacrificed in the name of this end to be the soul of Greece. And this requires her death as human. The king, as the visible manifestation of the divine principle, endorses values that are consciously recognized by the culture. In this culture, the feminine is reduced in value to being merely the object of masculine ends. Hence in the drama the women have no real power. Helen, as a beauty object, is seduced. Clytemnestra, as wife, is to obey her husband's rule. As a mother, she does have some rule in the home, but when it comes to saving her daughter's life, she is powerless. Iphigenia, as daughter, is to be sacrificed for the political power of the state. As she says to Agamemnon when she pleads for her life, "...my tears are my one magic; I'll use them, for I can weep."[7] But her pure innocence and her tears are of no avail when political power is the highest value. Thus, the culture's devaluation of the feminine, which King Agamemnon endorses, leads to the sacrifice of his daughter. And although Iphigenia is pure and noble and forgives her father when she sees the finality of his position, with her submission to her fate she finally acknowledges this devaluation of the feminine. She sacrifices herself for Greece and declares "One man is of more value than a host of women." Accepting the soul projection of her father, she says:

> ...let my father pace around the altar, following the sun. I come to give to all Hellenes deliverance and victory! Lead me, a maiden born to overthrow great Troy and all her people.[8]

Iphigenia, in becoming the soul of Greece, gives up her own feminine identity and the value of her tears "...since at the altar is no place for tears."[9] But although she submits and forgives, her mother, left in rage and grief, cannot forgive. And so the story of the family is continued when, in other plays, Clytemnestra murders Agamemnon to revenge Iphigenia's death, and in retribution of his father's death, the son, Orestes, murders his mother, Clytemnestra.[10]

The father-daughter sacrifice has its roots in the dominance of masculine power over the feminine. When the masculine is cut off from feminine values, when it does not allow the feminine principle to manifest itself in its own way out of its own center, when it does not allow the feminine its manifold number of forms but reduces it only to those which serve masculine ends, it loses its relation to the values of the feminine realm. It is then that the masculine becomes brute-like and sacrifices not only the outer woman but also its inner feminine side.

The image of this condition is expressed by Hexagram 12, "Standstill-Stagnation," found in the *I Ching*, the Chinese Taoist book of wisdom. The *I Ching*'s basic image of the cosmos and of human existence is based on the relationship between the feminine and masculine principles. When these two polarities are in harmonic relationship, there is the source for growth, spirit, and creativity—for the union of masculine and feminine wisdom. But when the feminine and masculine principles are out of harmony, there is the condition for chaos and destruction.

In Hexagram 12, "Standstill-Stagnation," the masculine principle (heaven) is above, and the feminine principle (earth) is below. About this relationship between the masculine and feminine, the *I Ching* says:

Heaven is above, drawing farther and farther away, while the earth below sinks farther into the depths. The creative powers are not in relation.... Heaven and earth are out of communion and all things are benumbed. What is above has no relation to what is below, and on earth confusion and disorder prevail.[11]

The *I Ching* goes on to say that with this constellation, mutual mistrust prevails in public life and fruitful activity is impossible because the relation between the two fundamental principles is wrong. Such is the relation between the masculine and feminine portrayed by Euripides in *Iphigenia in Aulis*. The disturbed relation between the masculine and feminine principles may exist within each person as well as between individuals, from the viewpoint of Jungian psychology. Every woman has a masculine side, often hidden in her unconscious psyche. Conversely, every man has a feminine side, which is frequently unconscious and unavailable to him. The task of personal growth for an individual is to become aware of this contrasexual side, to value it, and to express it consciously in the appropriate situation. When the contrasexual side is accepted and valued, it becomes a source of energy and inspiration, enabling a creative union of the masculine and feminine principles within the person as well as a creative relationship between men and women.

The feminine, when it is so devalued and suppressed, eventually becomes enraged and demands its due in primitive fashion, as Clytemnestra in revenge killed Agamemnon. The father-daughter sacrifice, then, not only affects the development of women but the inner development of men as well. Agamemnon is as injured and in despair, as unfree in life, as is his daughter, Iphigenia.

The split in the masculine between lust for beauty and lust for power and its corresponding split in the feminine between beautiful one (eternal girl) and dutiful one (armored amazon) is manifested in the drama between the warring brothers (Menelaus and Agamemnon) and the poorly related sisters (Helen and Clytemnestra). This fracture of opposites is entailed in the father-daughter wound. The masculine split into these two opposites in turn reduces the feminine

31

ideal to beauty and duty. Both brothers use women; the one for pleasure, the other for power. Iphigenia, personifying the feminine potential, initially protests this situation, but eventually submits to the power goal.

The sacrifice is made to Artemis, the virgin goddess of the hunt, because Agamemnon killed one of Artemis' stags without honoring her. In some myths Agamemnon even claimed to be a greater hunter than Artemis, who, in anger, stilled the winds and demanded Iphigenia's sacrifice.[12] Artemis was neglected by Agamemnon. Psychologically viewed, the neglect of a goddess shows that the aspect of the psyche which she represents has not been valued consciously. As a virgin goddess, Artemis symbolizes the virginal quality of *being at one-in-herself,* an inner attitude of feminine centeredness and independence.[13] One of Artemis' functions is to protect young girls at the age of puberty and teach them to be independent. This is what has been dishonored by Agamemnon and the prevailing cultural values. The feminine has had no effect on the masculine consciously. Ultimately, Agamemnon doesn't listen to either his wife or daughter. Neither has he allowed the feminine independence, nor does he respect one of the greatest of goddesses, Artemis. He values only his own power, taking what he wants, e.g., Artemis' stag. Perhaps Artemis demands this sacrifice to show Agamemnon what he loses by devaluing the feminine. To lose his daughter, a symbol of his own feminine potential, shows the consequences of his power attitude. If a man tramples over the feminine, he loses his relationship to it. So in one sense, the sacrifice to Artemis is necessary to honor this feminine independence.

Although *Iphigenia in Aulis* is a Greek drama written around 405 B.C., the same situation continues in our present day Western culture. The feminine is still reduced in many men's eyes to dutiful wife or beautiful mistress, or a variation on these themes. Many women still find themselves living for men and not for themselves. Some women, in reaction, have begun to break away and realize themselves in the professions. But too often in order to break out of the puella

dependency, they imitate the masculine model and so per-
petuate the devaluation of the feminine. In contrast, other
women who feel powerless and become enraged like Clytemnestra may overtly be dutiful to the system but covertly they
express their anger; for example, by eliminating sex, having
an affair in retaliation, charging up their husbands' credit
cards, drinking too much, becoming sick and hypochondria-
cal or depressed and suicidal, etc.

Perhaps the greatest wound the man suffers is not to
acknowledge his own wound—to be unable to weep. Many
fathers, under the illusion that they must always be right and
self-justified in order to maintain their control and authority,
and many men caught up in the power goals of control and
achievement in our technological age, find themselves in this
condition. They have lost the power of their tears and they
have failed to honor their own young, tender, feminine side.
Like Agamemnon, they have sacrificed their "inner daughter" in the name of their own power. Or like his brother,
Menelaus, they may have succumbed to the power of the
outer woman and have lost access to their own genuine inner
femininity. In either case, the independent feminine spirit is
not honored and is lost.

In many ways, *Iphigenia in Aulis* provides an image for
today: chaos and lust for power still prevail between the
sexes; spirit (the harmonic relation between the feminine
and masculine principles) still has not been found to be
moving effectively in the lives of most men and women. But
at least questions abound, and where there are questions,
there is quest, consciousness, and hope of breaking through
the inadequate existing patterns.

Many modern day Iphigenias exist in our culture, suffering from a narrow vision of femininity, a narrow vision
which is imbedded in the culture and frequently in personal
fathers and mothers as well. These women are often angry
and aware that the images allotted to women in our patriarchal culture have been influenced by men's inadequate
relation to femininity. Nevertheless, they feel trapped and
helpless.

Joan, a talented and attractive woman in her forties, is an example. She grew up feeling that the ideal woman should be like Helen—most beautiful, most desirable, a woman who could attract all men by her looks and who also could be and do whatever the man needed and desired. This image, supported by the culture, came also in part from her parents. Her mother, who suffered from a split within her own femininity, was cute, youthful, and dependent (the eternal girl), yet with an overface of the independent fighter (the armored amazon) who was unable to let go and enjoy the sexual relationship with her husband. Her father, frustrated in his marriage, loved his daughter, probably too much, so the daughter most likely received his unconscious wishes for a love relationship and also his guilt feelings about this.

Dreams provided images that helped her see some roles she had assumed but which were not really appropriate. In one dream Joan was relegated to a Cinderella position by her mother and had to clean up some dirty ashes. In some ways this was the unconscious message she got from her mother— that she was not as beautiful as her mother and that, as a dutiful daughter, her task was to clean up the inadequate relationship between her parents. The way Joan dealt with this was to become a mediator for her parents and to become very competent professionally. But inwardly she felt inferior because secretly she wanted to be "Helen," the woman for whom her father secretly hoped and the woman who was the cultural image of the times. To date, then be "pinned" by a fraternity man, and finally married just after college graduation was the goal for women of her milieu. When Joan was in her teens she felt out of phase with this image in terms of her own physical and emotional development. So peer pressure and the social dating system made her feel inferior. On the one hand she wanted cultural approval, yet she also hated that image for she knew it entailed a betrayal of women's genuine needs and potentialities. The men to whom she was attracted were consistently younger and boyish with whom she was in the mother role. These relationships didn't work since they didn't afford the mature relationship she wanted, and the men were often threatened and passive on the sexual level. In Joan's dreams her father frequently appeared as a morally judgmental figure who criticized her for having erotic relationships. So her connections with men who couldn't respond in a mature sexual way allowed her to avoid her father's possessiveness.

On the professional level she was seemingly a success. But even there she unconsciously bought into the masculine view of things when, instead of undertaking a creative project based on her own instinctive way of understanding feminine development, she undertook administrative projects. While she accomplished these quite well, they did not utilize her poetic talents to the utmost and kept her from exploring her creativity. She knew how to succeed in the male business world and her capacity for hard work and service gave her financial independence. But she was also tired of being so strong and she longed to be taken care of. On the conscious level she lived out a dutiful version of the armored Amazon, but secretly she longed to be Helen, the eternal girl desired by men. Like many women, she was also angry at the women who succeeded in this role.

Joan felt trapped by these two opposite images of the feminine. The dutiful servant-mother role was not fulfilling emotionally, and she was too independent and creative to become a mere image of man's unconscious wishes. A modern day Iphigenia, she felt sacrificed on the altar of the cultural father's disavowal of the independent feminine spirit. But unlike the Iphigenia in Euripides' play, ultimately Joan did not accept the cultural father's projections of femininity. On the concrete level she formed a women's group that explored divine feminine images existing in many cultures and myths. In her dreams she was approached by a mysterious and powerful female figure who invited her to ride an elephant, the royal animal who carried the Indian lords. This dream became a living image of the ecstatic experience of the feminine in which she found a source of innate power—a power that didn't need validation by an outer man or a patriarchal institution. For her the following poem by Mirabai, an Indian poetess, expressed the ecstatic experience of a woman who feels her own feminine centeredness and spirit and tries to express anew what it means to be a woman. As Robert Bly, a poet and translator of Mirabai has put it, "In her confidence, self-pity leaves."[14] The poem is called "Why Mira Can't Go Back To Her Old House":

> The colors of the Dark One have penetrated Mira's body;
>   other colors washed out.
> Making love with Krishna and eating little—those are my
>   pearls and carnelians.
> Chanting beads and the forehead streak—those are
>   my bracelets.
> That's enough feminine wiles for me. My teacher taught
>   me this.
> Approve me or disapprove me; I praise the Mountain
>   Energy night and day.
> I take the path that ecstatic human beings have taken
>   for centuries.
> I don't steal money, nor hit anyone—what will you charge
>   me with?
> I have felt the swaying of the elephant's shoulders...and
>   now you want me to climb on a jackass? Try
>   to be serious![15]

CHAPTER THREE

THE ETERNAL GIRL

I hate
this wretched willow soul of mine,
patiently enduring, plaited or twisted
by other hands.

                                        Karin Boye

Sleeping Beauty's father was a king who loved his daughter
dearly, but forgot to invite one of the oldest and most
powerful of the fairies to the celebration of his daughter's
christening. His forgetfulness of that feminine power resulted in 100 years of sleep and inactivity in the world for his
daughter. Cinderella's father allowed himself to be dominated by a very powerful second wife, so his daughter was
condemned by her jealous stepmother to live in rags and be
the scullery maid of the household. One man was seemingly
powerful, a king. The other was passive and ineffective. Both
daughters suffered, and both were relegated to passive and
inferior positions. This is the passive role which is one way
women live out the pattern of the "eternal girl." Both
Sleeping Beauty and Cinderella were finally saved by
princes, just as many women who have lived lives of passivity
have sought for safety and security in their marriages. Yet in
the end, most of these women feel they have betrayed
themselves.

Our culture has collaborated in this betrayal. Women have been praised for their compliancy, their adaptability, their gentleness, their youthful sweetness, their obedient cooperation with their husbands, who are "form to their matter." Women who live out their lives in this archetypal pattern of existence have simply remained fixated at the girlish level of development. Like Peter Pan, for a variety of reasons, they prefer not to grow up; they remain eternal girls. The advantages of this choice are understandable. It can be comfortable and exciting to be admired as a sweet young thing, to depend on someone stronger for important decisions, to luxuriate in romantic fantasies about the Prince Charming who can cut through Sleeping Beauty's hedge of thorns to rescue her, to flirt with possibility, to become the chameleon-like images of many a man's heart's delight, or even to shy away from life and live in an inner wishworld. But the disadvantages of such a feminine lifestyle abound too. In exchange for these benefits, the eternal girl often gives up her independence and settles for a passive, dependent life. Rather than developing herself on the personal and professional level, rather than working out her own identity, rather than finding out who she really is through the difficult task of self-transformation—the eternal girl usually gains her identity from the projections others have upon her. To name a few: the femme fatale, the good daughter, the charming wife and hostess, the beautiful princess, the *femme inspiratrice*, even the tragic heroine. Instead of assuming the strength and force of her potential and the responsibility that goes with it, the eternal girl dwells in weakness. Like a doll, she allows others to make of her life what they will.

In order to see better how the eternal girl functions, it is necessary first to look at some of the different ways in which this type of existence may manifest itself, and following that description to explore paths of transformation. The following examples are not intended in any way to be "types" or "categories" into which individual women might neatly fit, and in fact a particular woman might live out several of these lifestyles at different times and in different situations. They emerged spontaneously for me as just some of the different modes of behavior that such a woman might recognize in herself, and with that recognition gain some perspective on the way she leads her life.

1. THE DARLING DOLL

One frequent puella lifestyle is to lead the "darling" existence. Such a woman becomes the image her lover expects her to be, adapting herself to his fantasies of the feminine. Outwardly she may appear secure and successful, and like a powerful princess she may be the envy of many a woman's secret wish. But inwardly her identity is fragile and insecure, for in continually posing for others she does not know who she really is. As in the movie *Darling*, she is like a photographer's model whose identity is determined and objectified by the eye behind the camera. She is virtually a doll, a puppet.

How many women have lived most of their married life in this way, being a charming companion and hostess for their husbands, only to find themselves in the midst of a divorce in mid-life, with little or no personal strength and development?

Ibsen's play *A Doll's House* shows this pattern very clearly. The main character, Nora, is a charming wife who dresses up for her husband, Torvald, and does whatever he wants her to do. She is his doll, his little plaything, his "shy little darling," his "little squirrel," his "little lark," his "little spendthrift," "little songbird," "little featherbrain," and so on—all pet names which he calls her. From her husband's point of view, Nora is to be protected since she is incapable of being practical, handling money, making decisions, and being responsible. Although he criticizes her father for these same boyish qualities, in Nora he finds them desirable and charming. For example, he says to her:

Just lean on me; I will advise you and direct you. I shouldn't be a man if this womanly helplessness did not actually give you a double attractiveness in my eyes...I will serve as will and conscience both to you.[1]

What her husband doesn't know is that Nora had actually provided for him by borrowing money when he was sick to pay for a trip essential to his health. Nora, knowing that her husband, with his "manly independence," would be too proud and humiliated to accept this from her, kept it a secret. Over the years she managed, by working quietly, to pay off the loan. But to get the loan she had to sign her father's name since he was too sick himself at the time. The crisis and confrontation for Nora comes when the money lender threatens to expose her in this forgery. At first she tries to do everything to keep her husband from knowing and uses all her "little squirrel" charm to do so. But gradually she realizes that in doing this she is really hiding who she is from him, hiding not only her mistake but also her competence and strength. As this realization becomes clearer she decides to let the whole thing come out into the open. When her husband finds out and his public image is at stake, he becomes furious and is confirmed in his view that she is irresponsible. In anger he says to her:

> Do you understand what you have done?...all your father's want of principle has come out in you. No religion, no morality, no sense of duty....[2]

Hearing this Nora knows she can no longer continue to play a role for her husband and that she must stand up for herself and confront him. When the threat of exposure from the money lender is withdrawn and her husband forgives her, since now it has no serious consequence for him, she has the chance to revert to her doll's role. But she realizes that his change of attitude has come only from externals and that he still sees her as a child. And so she confronts him, saying that this is the first time in eight years of marriage that they have had a serious conversation. She says:

I have been greatly wronged, Torvald—first by father and then by you. You have never loved me. You have only thought it pleasant to be in love with me. When I was at home with father, he told me his opinions about everything, and so I had the same opinions; and if I differed from him I concealed the fact because he would not have liked it. He called me his doll-child, and he played with me just as I used to play with my dolls. And when I came to live with you—I mean that I was simply transferred from father's hands into yours. You arranged everything according to your taste, and so I got the same tastes as you—or else I pretended to. I am really not quite sure which.[3]

For Nora this insight brings with it the realization that she does not really know who she is because she has always been dependent on a man. She understands that she must stand alone to understand herself and that she must learn to form her own values and opinions rather than accept the views of others, or of the collective. In the play her final decision is to leave her husband and children and strike out on her own.

While this may appear to be a radical solution (especially since Ibsen wrote the play in 1879), even now women not infrequently feel the necessity to leave their families and go off on their own. It is most important, I feel, to see the meaning behind this kind of act, i.e., the realization that it is not enough to exist as a function of husband's wishes and projections, and that it is necessary to find out for oneself who one really is. Imagine how angry such a woman must feel at the shock of seeing that her life is not really her own, that she has been directed from above like a puppet. One of the chief tasks here is to avoid indulging in anger and merely acting out resentment bitterly and revengefully. It may very well be that one's father, husband, and men in general by their projections have contributed to such an inadequate view of the feminine. But reaction to such projections via blame only perpetuates the projection of passivity and dependency. Moreover, there may be a shadow aspect to be dealt with, for very often behind the pliant wife is a powerful woman who manipulates her husband covertly, as Nora does. The task then is to begin to form one's values and views of life and to consciously accept one's power, using it creatively and openly.

One woman who had lived out the first part of her life as a "darling doll" had a dream in which there were a series of dolls all lined up. In this case the dolls were male dolls dressed exactly alike and she could choose any doll she wished. The dream helped her realize that just as she was a doll for men, having no identity of her own but conforming instead to men's fantasies of her, so men were "dolls" for her too. Her relationships to men were as impersonal as theirs to her. This impersonal relationship typified her first marriage and repeated a pattern she had had with her father, a powerful business tycoon. In the second part of her life she chose to develop her own abilities and met a man who appreciated her development as well as her charm and beauty.

2. THE GIRL OF GLASS

Another form the puella existence may take is to be shy and fragile and out of life, often living in a world of fantasy. Tennessee Williams' play *The Glass Menagerie* shows this very poignantly. Laura, the protagonist, is a typical puer's daughter. Her father, a charming and romantic figure, abandoned the family years ago, never to be heard from again. The narrator of the play, who is Laura's brother, describes him, pointing to the larger than life picture of this gallantly smiling father which hangs on the living room wall just left of the archway, suggesting the enormous unconscious influence he exerts:

> This is our father who left us a long time ago. He was a telephone man who fell in love with long distances; he gave up his job with the telephone company and skipped the light fantastic out of town.... The last we heard of him was a picture postcard from Mazatlan, on the Pacific coast of Mexico,

containing a message of two words: 'Hello—Goodbye!' and no address.[4]

Laura's mother, who works constantly in martyr fashion, displaying her dissatisfaction with the missing puer father-husband, lives in a fantasy world which clings to the past, and projects her own wishes upon her daughter. She wants her daughter to be the "belle of the ball," as she had been before marriage. But Laura is quite different from her mother, although she lives in a private fantasy world, too. Hers is a world of old phonograph records which her father had left behind and a menagerie of tiny glass animals whose lives she constantly creates. Her favorite is a unicorn, a wonderful imaginary horned horse and a favorite with maidens from time immemorial. The glass menagerie and her father's old phonograph records are the world in which she lives, and not the extraverted, practical, social world of her mother.

The fragile glass animals are an image of Laura's own fragility and remoteness from life, and the music and the old phonograph records are a nostalgic reminder that while her father is not physically present, he is there emotionally. Laura is also crippled, one leg slightly shorter than the other and in a brace. The crippling is symbolic of the psychic crippling inherent in her family situation. The crippling shows psychologically in Laura's extreme shyness and lack of self-confidence, which is so severe that she can finish neither high school nor a business school to which her mother has sent her.

Laura's situation is not so different, though the details may vary, from that of many women who spend their lives in fantasy, perhaps with a "ghostly lover" or mystical dream—unable to get into the world and relate to men—enclosed in the glass mountain of their own fantasy. But Laura is lucky. Like Sleeping Beauty's prince, someone from outside the family situation enters her world, even though only for an evening. At the mother's insistence, her brother invites a friend, Jim, to dinner, a man whom Laura had admired in

43

high school as a hero. Warm and outgoing, he provides a relation to life which her father had not provided and which her brother cannot provide because he must free himself. When Jim comes to visit, Laura is at first so shy that she becomes faint and cannot eat with the others. But later in the evening Jim talks to her and is able to enter her world. Her shyness begins to dissolve in his warmth and she shows him her glass menagerie, and especially the unicorn. Sensing that her shyness is due to a lack of self-confidence, he tells her she doesn't have enough faith in herself, that she must acknowledge the fact that she is a superior person, and that she has magnified her crippled leg a hundred times. Bringing her a bit into his world, he invites her to dance. At first she says she can't dance, but his encouragement enables her to try. Inadvertently while they are dancing, the unicorn is jolted from the table and the horn is broken off, leaving an almost ordinary horse. Attached as she is to her unicorn, Laura might have retreated farther from Jim and what he represents. But knowing somewhere in her heart that the unicorn is extinct and really not appropriate, she accepts the event, even saying that the unicorn will feel less freakish now and gives it to Jim as a parting gift. Although it turns out that Jim is engaged to be married, this experience of understanding from a warm, caring man who is related to the outer world brings Laura a step further. For now she has danced and given her unicorn to another human being—both a venture into the realm of life and action. Transformation, in the case of Laura, is initiated through the masculine, which up to this point has been lacking. But it also takes the initiation of Laura to respond to him—to take the leap of faith to risk and trust.

In contrast to the previous pattern where the father projected too much upon the daughter and the task was to break from the projections of the father and husband, this pattern deals with an absent father. For Laura there was no relation to the masculine, no influence actively and consciously coming from the father, and no relationship to the world provided. It is true that the mother tries to do this in

44

her fashion, but she also lives in a fantasy world and doesn't really understand her daughter. With no masculine projections or relationship, Laura creates her own world, a fantasy life which compensates for being cut off from the outer world. Many women live out this pattern, but ordinarily we don't hear about them because they hide themselves. But when their fantasy world breaks down through a confrontation with reality, they frequently come into therapy.

One way of hiding out from the practical, extraverted world is to retreat into the world of books—especially poetry and fantasy. One of my clients did this and as a child actually had a glass menagerie of animals. She grew up very poor, had an absent father, and every cent she could get went into her glass animal collection and books. As a child her favorite book was *Heidi*, the story of an orphan who went to live in the Alps with her cynical, reclusive grandfather. But Heidi was an outgoing child whose warmth and spontaneity brought life and love to her grandfather and also to a bedridden sick girl. Heidi was a part of this woman's personality, a side that had been squelched in childhood, but finally emerged as she gained more confidence. Ultimately she dared to write herself, and in that way came out before the public eye. Then she had to face the lecture circuit and had many "girl of glass" anxiety fantasies about fainting in front of the audience. Every time she did this was traumatic but she took the risk and in this way was able to bring her inner world into connection with the outer world, thus sharing her special vision with others.

3. THE HIGH FLYER: DONNA JUANA

The woman who flies high is another puella pattern. This puella lives by impulse, is free as the wind and exuberant. She seems to be spontaneous and free, leading a wild and exciting life, going with the whim of the moment and with whatever is happening. Soaring away, she lives in the realm of possibilities. This lifestyle tends to be ethereal as well, magically appearing and disappearing like a cloud that forms for a moment and disappears. Timeless and "spacy," this puella usually has a poor relationship to boundaries, to limits, to the practical order, to the corporeal realm, and to time. Her life is largely undirected and open to the synchronous. Such women are often intuitive, with artistic or mystical tendencies, living easily in imagination and close to the unconscious and archetypal realms. They share this in common with the shy and fragile puellas, but unlike the shy ones they are not fearful and retiring, nor are they hidden from the world. Rather, they are up there adventurously floating along in rarified air, often seeking the thrills of danger.

Anaïs Nin, herself a puer's daughter, has beautifully described this type of existence in her novel *A Spy in the House of Love.* As the title implies, the main character, Sabina, lives the life of a spy. Uncommitted and deceitful in relationships, she must live like a spy to be free to move on at any time and is constantly on guard against revealing herself and thus exposing her various deceptions. Like a kaleidoscope, she changes personalities and stories with the rapidity of one obsessed. Sabina is married to a stable man who functions as a kind father and whom she needs as the one solid point in her life. But her feelings toward him are more like "an adolescent escaping from home for some forbidden games." Sabina cannot bear the exigencies of ordinary, daily life and rebels against them. Life's limitations and resting points are to Sabina like a prison. Boundaries, identifications, houses, any sort of commitment—all these she feels mold her into a static place without any hope of change. She describes herself: *"I want the impossible, I want to fly all the time, I destroy ordinary life, I run towards all the danger of love..."*[5]

The moon and not the sun is Sabina's special lighting source and her special planet. The night world and the unconscious are her domain. At sixteen she took moonbaths because everyone else took sunbaths and because she had heard they were dangerous. Like the moon, which keeps half of itself in darkness, so does she, living many mysterious lives

46

and loves and eluding clocktime by her dream-like extension into the infinite. Activated by the moonrays, Sabina imagines she knows the moonlife which is "homeless, childless, free lovers, not ever tied to each other." It is to this ideal that she is drawn.

In order to have this free, adventurous life, Sabina deceives her husband by telling him she is working as an actress and must be here and there on tour. In many ways she is an actress, composing a new face and costume to meet each day and each new lover. But unlike a professional actress, the roles never end, for the men for whom she has played have taken them for real and could be angry and feel betrayed if they knew the truth. For Sabina there is no respite from the stage and no essential Sabina to whom she can return.

Sabina realizes that it is her father who is "walking within her, directing her steps" in the feminine form of his Don Juan existence. Like Sabina, her father depended on her mother's loyalty and groundedness in domestic life as a base from which he left for a multitude of amorous adventures. She questions herself:

> Was it Sabina now rushing into her own rituals of pleasure, or was it her father within her, his blood guiding her into amorousness, dictating her intrigues, he who was inexorably woven with her by threads of inheritance she could never separate again to know which one was Sabina, which one her father whose role she had assumed by alchemy of mimetic love.
> Where was Sabina?[6]

This question, "Where is Sabina?" obtrudes more and more into her consciousness. Guilt, shame, and anxiety begin to overtake her and she realizes that her love anxieties are not so different from those of an addict or a gambler; i.e., the same compulsion and irresistible impulse and then the same depression and guilt which follow and then once more the compulsion. Sabina's addiction is love, but the end effect is the same. She feels the dispersion, the desperation, the weakness at the center. She looks at the sky arched overhead and realizes that for her it offers no cathedral protection, only a "limitless vastness to which she could not cling." Sabina weeps and asks to be held so she will not continue to race from one love to another, so she will not continue to be dispersed and disrupted.

In desperation during the deep of night, she makes an anonymous phone call to a stranger, seeking help. The man who answers is a lie detector, symbolizing Sabina's inner possibility to detect her own self-deception and achieve a higher level of consciousness and responsibility. The lie detector confronts her, asking her what she wants to confess and telling her that she is probably her own most severe judge. Sabina asks the lie detector to set her free from the guilt she suffers, a guilt and imprisonment which is paradoxically born of the limitless freedom she has sought. But he tells her that only she can set herself free and that will only come when she is able to love. When she tries to justify that she *has* loved by mentioning her many lovers, he points out that she was only in love with her projections, e.g., the crusaders who fought her battles, the handsome Don Juan princes, the judges continuing her parents' role. Rather than relating to them as individuals and seeing them as they were in reality, she dressed them in costumes of the various myths she wanted to live out.

For Sabina the change can come only with the tears of acknowledgement for her deception of self and others. Up to now she has been trying to elude her guilt and find self-justification for her lack of commitment and recognition of limitations. To recognize that continuity exists in the tension between movement and permanence is something she needs to learn. And this recognition does finally come to her as she listens to Beethoven's Quartets, music to which she weeps in acknowledgement.

The difficulty for this type of puella is that she tries to live totally in possibility and ignores the limitations and realities of others and herself. But what she needs to do is accept the boundaries and commit herself to something. Accepting the paradox of finitude and possibility is her way of resolution; the Beethoven Quartets express this paradox in their composition, i.e., they express transcendence contained. Creating via the various art forms is one way to this end. For example, Anaïs Nin transformed the puella existence in herself through her writing, giving form to her intuitions and thus bringing possibility and actuality together.

Recently a young, vivacious woman called to make an appointment. When I asked her why she wanted to start therapy she said she was in love with a man who also loved her, but he had told her that unless she could "settle down" and get a sense of her own values, he couldn't consider her as a real partner. Her aim was to define herself instead of dispersing herself in relationships as she tended to do. Her pattern was to fly from man to man, and she felt her value by both the number of men she slept with, as well as their differing nationalities. At the age of nineteen she had already slept with thirty or so men and from as many countries. She was very spontaneous and would often go off at a moment's notice with a stranger she had just met on the street. When I asked her to write down her dreams and bring them to me, she usually forgot or else they were written on old bills, toilet paper, whatever she had around at the moment. Developmentally, her mother wanted her to be a "virgin" and her father wasn't around emotionally. First she became her mother's pet, "a good girl," then rebelled and lived out her mother's unacknowledged side. At one point she had a dream that she was a French poodle, her mother's favorite pet, and when her mother gave her a dog treat that was filled with poison, at first she swallowed it, but then vomited it out. This is what she had done psychologically. She wanted to be her mother's pet, but vomited out the "virgin" treat. The result was that she flipped to the opposite and slept around. Her father wasn't around enough to give her a sense of her own feminine value. This woman's task was to see that she was rebelling against her mother via her flighty life, but that this also kept her from relating to the man whom she loved.

4. THE MISFIT

Still another mode of the puella is the woman who, because of shame over her father, is rejected by and/or rebels against society. This woman may be identified with her father and remain attached to him in a positive way, so that when society rejects him, she rejects society. Or, it may be that initially she rejected her father, but then there emerges the shadow side from the unconscious and she lives out that pattern anyway. In such a family situation, the mother often takes a self-righteous role and becomes the critic of the "bad father." If the daughter shows any modes of behavior similar to that of the father, the mother will often castigate her, threatening her with the same doom as her father's fate. Unless the daughter follows the "good advice" of the mother (most likely in that case taking an Amazon pattern), she may rebel and repeat the father's pattern, acting out his self-destructive side.

Dostoyevsky has described this pattern in many of his feminine characters who have had addictive fathers of one sort or another. And it seems to me that these puellas often have a Dostoyevskyan "Underground Man" inside them who cynically refuses to assume the possibility of help, who refuses to change both himself and the society which has rejected him. These women are likely to waste their lives in inertial passivity, perhaps taking the route of alcohol or drug addiction, prostitution, suicidal fantasies, or perhaps falling into addictive love relationships. Or they might also marry a man like the father and waste away in depression and masochism of an unfulfilled life and relationship. Somehow, like Persephone, these women have been drawn into Pluto's dark underworld and there they remain with little or no ego strength and animus development to help them out.

Arthur Miller has described this type of puella existence in his play *After the Fall*, modelling the character Maggie partially on his ex-wife, Marilyn Monroe. Initially Maggie appears to be a very attractive figure to Quentin, the male protagonist, since she is innocent, sexually open, seemingly non-defensive, and admires him. When Quentin first meets her, Maggie is very vulnerable to the advances of men and seems not to have an inner discretion about who will hurt her or be dangerous for her. She also sees Quentin as a god-like figure and feels her own self-value comes from his valuing of her. Maggie, too, has had no positive father influence, since her father left when she was an infant, even denying that he was the father. And so she grew up as a bastard. Her mother, ashamed of this situation, became very moral and rejecting of Maggie. When Quentin comes along, Maggie projects upon him the power to save her, a projection which he finds irresistible. But along with this power goes the responsibility for her life, and that, too, she gives to Quentin. Secretly, Maggie believes she is worth nothing, even calling herself "Miss None" when she registers in hotels. She says:

> I could register in the hotel as Miss None...No—'n-o-n-e' like nothing. I made it up once cause I can never remember a fake name, so I just have to think of nothing and that's me.[7]

With such low self-esteem and self-respect, Maggie needs to be adored as a compensation. Initially, Quentin (who identifies with the power to save her that Maggie projects upon him) succeeds in convincing Maggie of his adoration. But eventually, no matter what Quentin does, Maggie becomes jealous; because she has no self-valuing to ground her, she falls into despair and depression at every suspicion that Quentin is not totally devoted to her. To escape she turns to alcohol, an addiction that symbolizes her dependency and need for constant and total acceptance. It also reconfirms her fears that she really is "Miss None," the lowest of the low, a victim of society. And it enables her to release her cynicism and aggression, which had been hiding behind her innocence, and this she vents against Quentin. At the same time she threatens suicide, implying that Quentin is the only one who could save her life. But Quentin, finally realizing that it is not in his power to save her, and that she alone can save herself, confronts her and says:

Do you see it, Maggie? Right now? You're trying to make me
the one who does it to you?...But now I'm going away; so
you're not my victim anymore. It's just you and your hand...
You eat those pills to blind yourself, but if you could only say,
"I have been cruel," this frightening room would open. If you
could say, "I have been kicked around, but I have been just as
inexcusably vicious to others, called my husband idiot in
public, I have been utterly selfish despite my generosity, I
have been hurt by a long line of men, but I have cooperated
with my persecutors...[8]

But at this point Maggie is so identified with being a victim
that she cannot hear him and eventually she commits suicide.
Absolutizing her own innocence and victimization, she refuses to see that she is not only a victim but also persecutor,
both of herself and Quentin. She refuses to acknowledge that
she too is guilty; thus neither can she forgive nor live.

The paradox at the bottom of this puella pattern is that
despite the real humiliation, shame, and rejection of past
history, resulting in self-identification with the victim and
worthless one, the way of redemption is to fight this identification rather than compulsively living out the shame and
repeating the pattern of rejection. This requires accepting
that one is both innocent and guilty, and that within oneself
exists both the power to destroy and to save. The task is to
transform the cynical attitude, despair, and rejection into an
attitude of hope and to consciously affirm oneself and life.

An example of this transforming attitude is in Fellini's
film *Nights of Cabiria*. Cabiria is a streetwalker, a prostitute, who has been victimized by men from childhood on.
Under hypnosis at a show, she inadvertently reveals her past
history with men as well as the fact that she has some savings.
After the show a man comes up to her and says he has fallen
in love with her. At first disbelieving, Cabiria finally believes
him and they plan to get married. For the first time in her life
it seems that she has found a man she can trust. After the
marriage, the couple go to a beautiful honeymoon spot on a

cliff high above the ocean. As Cabiria in all her happiness blissfully looks at the ocean, her husband tries to push her off the cliff, snatches her money, which is everything she has, and runs away. Cabiria is able to save her life but not her life's possessions. After this traumatic event, Cabiria starts to walk back to the city. A curious mixture of people, all outsiders, happen to be passing by, singing and playing music. Cabiria, still in the aftermath of this latest, most horrible treatment, at first just looks at them. Rejected and humiliated as she was, it would have been very easy to refuse all human connection and remain the outsider. But suddenly she smiles and joins their singing, thus accepting life, even with all of its horrors and tragedies. Her smile and song are a courageous affirmation of life despite tremendous vicissitudes, a laugh that overcomes defeat. Humor and acceptance of life's paradoxes seem to be the essential key here, together with a child-like resiliency and faith that is ready to go on despite everything.

A frequent "misfit" issue currently in our society comes up for many women who have chosen the lesbian or bisexual lifestyle. Among many of my clients I find tremendous guilt around this issue. Frequently the guilt occurs when the woman has had a "bad" father. If she chooses the lesbian mode, she is an "outsider" like her father. If the mother criticizes her for this, then the daughter feels bad like the father; an unconscious identity with him takes place, and then she is not free to choose her sexual preference, be it heterosexual, bisexual, or lesbian. One woman had a dream where a grandfather figure told her that her therapist had diagnosed her as a "social deviant." One of her issues was to be able to accept herself and give up the good girl role she had played as a child, particularly as her mother's darling daughter. This involved her trust that she could be who she needed to be without moral judgment coming from her therapist. She needed to disidentify from the negative image of herself which came from her father's behavior and her mother's moral judgment.

5. THE PUELLA'S DESPAIR

The foregoing patterns are not intended to be "types," but rather phenomenological descriptions of four basically different modes of puella existence. Nor are they exclusive of one another—most women are likely at one time or another to recognize each pattern. But it may be that one of these patterns predominates. Moreover, some of the different patterns have features in common. For example, the rebellious aspect is often part of the woman who flies high, as it was with Sabina. And the overly extreme emphasis on receiving the admiration of men can be a feature not only of the darling doll, but of the high flyer and misfit as well. The emphasis on imagination shows up in the shy, fragile puella as well as the high flyer, although the high flyer lives out her imagination in the world while the girl of glass retreats from the world into imagination.

Common to all of these puella patterns is a clinging to either absolutized innocence or absolutized guilt which are two sides of the same coin and which foster dependence on another for affirming or condemning. Hence there is an avoidance of responsibility for one's own existence, a lack of decision-making and discrimination, leaving these activities up to the other. There is also a poor relationship to limit and boundary—either in refusing to accept limits (e.g., the woman who flies and the misfit) or in "limitlessly" accepting limits (e.g., the shy recluse and the darling doll). Both these tendencies absolutize possibility and ignore necessity insofar as the relation to limit and boundary is distorted. The puella lives out her life in the possible, avoiding the actuality of commitment. Kierkegaard has described this mode of existence as an aspect of despair in *Sickness Unto Death* as follows:

> Now if possibility outruns necessity, the self runs away from itself, so that it has no necessity whereto it is bound to return—then this is the despair of possibility. The self becomes an abstract possibility which tires itself out with floundering in

the possible, but does not budge from the spot, nor get to any spot, for precisely the necessary is the spot; to become oneself is precisely a movement at the spot. To become is a movement from the spot, but to become oneself is a movement at the spot.

Possibility then appears to the self ever greater and greater, more and more things become possible, because nothing becomes actual. At last it is as if everything were possible—but this is precisely when the abyss has swallowed up the self.[9]

As Kierkegaard points out, dwelling in the possible can take one in two major directions, either toward wishful yearning or toward the melancholy fantastic. It seems to me that the darling doll and the high flyer tend toward the former while the girl of glass and the misfit tend toward the latter. But all cases result in an inability to act. For genuine action, the synthesis and integration of both possibility and necessity are required, and it is this synthesis, according to Kierkegaard, which is one of the grounding aspects of selfhood.

The central issue for the puella is to assert herself as who she really is, since her tendency has been to gain her identity (or lack of identity) from others. She has allowed herself to become an "object," to live out an identity that is not her own, thus congealing the flow of mystery which she is. The irony is that her vague and vacuous chameleon identity, her continual dwelling in possibility, may be a mistaken attempt to connect with the mystery in her soul, i.e., "to be mysterious." But genuine mystery cannot be caught and fixed in that way. What is really required to relate to one's mystery is to discriminate objectively what one's own potentialities and limitations really are and to actualize that synthesis. The puella needs to accept her potentiality for strength and to develop it in order to make this actualization, and to commit herself to her own unique mysterious being.

The basis of the puella problem lies in what Kierkegaard calls "The Despair of Weakness: the despair of not willing to be oneself." In this form of despair one realizes that one is not in relationship with the self, but feels too weak to choose the

55

self. Hence the despair is over one's weakness, one's inability to choose a more meaningful way of life. The puella's ego-adaptation has been precisely to be weak—to be passive and play the part others want her to be. Even the inflated puella, the "high flyer," remains weak since she doesn't actualize her possibilities but only plays with them. Thus she never becomes a powerful figure in the world. Living perpetually in possibility as the puella tends to do fosters weakness because she never accomplishes anything. As Kierkegaard describes it so well, she is swallowed up in the abyss of possibility. The puella, once she becomes conscious of her pattern, realizes she is trapped, stopped short in her development. For she, too, has something to contribute to the world, although she has not yet found the way to do this. And how frustrating this is—knowing one has something to contribute but not being able to do it. That is the "despair of weakness." And that tension can lead to suicide, withdrawal, adaptation, or rebellion. But it can also lead to transformation.

TOWARDS TRANSFORMATION

The first step of the way in transforming this pattern is to become conscious that one is out of relation to the self, to know and feel there is more in oneself, a higher power beyond ego-impulses to which one has not related and which frequently is revealed in dreams. And this consciousness brings with it suffering and the necessary second step of accepting that suffering. And then there is a final step, a most surprising one after all this—the realization that, despite our weakness, we have within us strength as well, an access to that higher power. In Kierkegaard's analysis, higher consciousness of the despair of weakness brings with it the realization that dwelling in weakness is really a form of defiance, i.e., an indulgence which refuses to accept the strength which is already there as a potentiality in the Self.

The final step, as I see it, is to *accept* the strength of the Self. This acceptance involves consciousness and choice, but a choice which is not to be confused with ego-willpower. It is the choice at the very basis of our being to accept the power of the Self. For Kierkegaard this is ultimately an act of faith requiring all the strength of receptivity.

Psychologically considered, the first step of conscious recognition enables the seeing of the pattern. Conscious naming is a first step of freedom from the negative structure. The fairy tale "Rumpelstiltskin" shows this clearly.[10] In the fairy tale there is a puer father, a poor miller, who to make himself appear important tells the king that he has a beautiful daughter who can spin straw into gold. The king asks that the girl be put to the test, but the daughter does not know how to fulfill this task which came out of the fanciful imagination of her father. And so she weeps. Then in comes a little man who says he will do the task if she will give him something for it. First she promises a necklace and he spins the straw into gold. Then the king demands more gold, and she promises the little man a ring and again he does the task. Again the king demands she spin straw into gold for a third time, and, if she fulfills the task, he will take her as his wife. And again comes the little man who says he will do it if she promises him her first child. Since the girl thinks this may never happen and since she feels helpless, she makes the promise, and the little man performs the task. And so the girl becomes a queen and within a year has a beautiful child. Although she has forgotten about her promise, the little man has not, and now he demands the child she has promised him, unless she can find out his name. So far there is a typical puella strucure: A puer father who, out of his own weakness and lack of actualization, puts his daughter into a realm of possibility she can't handle; her feeling of helplessness before the situation; and then an unrealistic promise to a limiting inner figure or pattern who helps out in the moment but demands and may take away the greatest value in the end. In the fairy tale the girl finds out the little man's name through a messenger she has sent into the world to inquire far and wide what names there might be. And when she tells the little man his name is Rumpelstiltskin, he is so enraged to have been found out that he stamps his foot in the ground and can't get it out again and then tears himself in two. By naming, she is able to keep her child, symbolic of her true potentiality, and depotentiate the old limiting complex, symbolized by Rumpelstiltskin. In the same way, by naming the pattern which comes from a mode of reaction to a negligent father development, one can loosen its grip and be free for a more genuine way of existence. Naming the pattern will give the puella the perspective and distance she needs and an insight into why she has remained fixated in her development. The naming also requires an active search, symbolized by the messenger sent out into the world. Naming is an active process.

The next task implied in understanding the despair of weakness is a conscious acceptance of the suffering involved in the puella's life up to now; that is, an acceptance that the suffering is actually meaningful. Part of the puella problem is to feel one's weakness and dependence and to see oneself as a victim. But if one identifies as victim, one in effect disclaims responsibility and acts as the innocent girl. So real understanding of the weakness and acceptance of the suffering involves facing the shadow, that part of oneself that is denied. Along with the sweet girlish innocence often goes nasty manipulation. The darling doll and the high flyer may secretly put men down because they are so easily seduced and manipulated by feminine charms (e.g., "the woman behind the man"). The misfit manipulates through her self-destructive threats and the power projections on others through which she has ensnared them. The girl of glass makes others feel helpless before her fragility and sensitivity so they may feel they are clumsy oafs, like bulls in a china shop. The shadow of the puella is tied up with power—a power which she has not truly and responsibly accepted. Oftentimes this power has been taken over by another figure in the psyche, a perverted old man, a mean and bad tempered figure like Rumpelstiltskin. And this figure, too, must be confronted. Part of accepting the suffering entails a battle with this figure which, as I see it, is, at a deeply spiritual level, a battle with the devil. When there is a deep wound in the psyche, the negative forces assume a demonic character and must be confronted as such. In Kierkegaard's analysis, when one becomes conscious that one's indulgence in weakness is really a defiant refusal to accept one's strength, a refusal to accept the grace of God, one realizes that the refusal to accept strength is demonic, a prideful clinging to one's own ego-power. Part of accepting the suffering is to realize one has been in the grips of the devil.

The final issue is to accept the strength that is there and to hold on to it rather than giving up and following the usual puella patterns of fleeing or withdrawing or adapting or rebelling. Of course, this is the very issue for the puella—just what she finds so hard to do. But if she has already become conscious of the negative patterns in which she has been trapped and if she has accepted suffering and the battle with the devil, she becomes involved in accepting the power and strength of consciousness and choice. This, however, is a gradual process and may take many years, as it took seven years in the fairy tale of "The Handless Maiden," to counteract the effects of the devil (brought on by inadequate fathering) and to unite with a king. Her way involved patiently waiting in the forest, in the knowledge that this is what she had to do. Thus, patient, understanding waiting seems a key and finalization to the process.

The question still remains: how does the process of transformation start? Where does the puella first find the revelation of the strength that is in her? The strength is there, but she must be open to it. This revelation may come to her in a variety of ways. It might come in the form of a relationship as it did for Laura in *The Glass Menagerie,* and as it did for Maggie in *After the Fall,* although Maggie chose to refuse it. It might come in the form of an outer crisis, of being found out in one's weakness (or in one's strength), as it did for Nora in *The Doll House.* Or it might come via an inner crisis, as it did for Sabina in *A Spy in the House of Love.* It might also come from a synchronous happening, as it did when Cabiria met the group of singers in *Nights of Cabiria.* Still another way is for the strength to show itself via a dream image, which can be held and talked to further in active imagination. Or it might even come in a strong emotion, a fit of rage, in a fight in which one really feels one's strength. The opportunities are all around. So the secret is in being alert and open to them.

Ultimately, what is demanded of the puella in the process of self-transformation is to give up her clinging to girlish dependence, innocence, and powerlessness and to accept the strength which is already there—to really value herself. For if she accepts her power and strength, then her girlish innocence will show itself as youthful, feminine élan and vigor, as the spontaneity and openness to new experience that makes creativity and fruitful relationship possible.

CHAPTER FOUR

THE ARMORED AMAZON

Being thought innocuous rouses some women to frenzy;
They try to be ugly by aping the ways of men
And succeed. Swearing, sucking cigars and scorching
                                                the bedspread,
Slopping straight shots, eyes blotted, vanity-blown
In the expectation of glory: she writes like a man!
                                                Carolyn Kizer

The Amazon culture, according to legend, devalued men by
eliminating them from all ruling positions. Often the Amazon
women made men slaves and used them as an impersonal
means of procreation. In this way they eliminated the father
as a personal figure by keeping him anonymous. The daughters were usually exalted while the infant boys were often
crippled and used for domestic service. Thus, the male
figures were depotentiated both physically and socially. Men
were not needed in this society because the Amazons took
over all the male functions. They were reputed for being
conquerors and huntresses, wild women warriors, courageous and daring horsewomen. And they trained their
daughters in this pattern. Legend says that they even
removed their right breast so they could shoot arrows more
effectively. According to some accounts, the Amazons were
daughters of Ares, the god of warfare and aggression, hence

61

their war-like approach to life and their stance as "warrior women."

The figure of the Amazon can be a mythological expression of the way many women live their lives in an unconscious identification with the masculine. If a woman has had a father who has been negligent or irresponsible, i.e., not emotionally present as a father for his daughter, one frequent pattern is to react against him. In such cases the daughter is likely to reject the father (and even men in general) on the conscious level since she has experienced him as unreliable. When this psychological reaction occurs, the tendency is to identify unconsciously with the masculine principle. In contrast to the woman whose principle ego identity is to be a helpless girl—to live out a puella pattern—the Amazon woman identifies with masculine strength and power.

Similarly, if the cultural representatives of the father principle have been irresponsible towards the valuation of the feminine, a reaction against such an irresponsible authority seems inevitable. This pattern seems to be prevalent in our contemporary culture.

The modern Amazon woman has been described by June Singer in her book, *Androgyny* as follows:

> The Amazon is a woman who has taken on characteristics that are generally associated with the masculine disposition but, rather than integrating the "masculine" aspects that could make her strong *as woman*, she identifies with the power aspect of the "masculine." At the same time she renounces the capacity to relate lovingly, a quality that has traditionally been associated with the feminine...so that the Amazon woman who takes on the power as she negates the capacity to relate lovingly to other human beings becomes one-sided, and consequently she is the victim of the very attribute she has tried to overwhelm.[1]

Often a woman who has taken on a masculine identity in reaction to an irresponsible father is cut off from life by virtue of her need for power, her defensive self-protection from that which she cannot control. In effect, she is trapped in an "Amazon armor," a powerful persona which may not correspond to her basic personality since it has been formed out of a reaction and not out of her inner feminine center. Quite often she is cut off from her feeling and receptivity and the strength of her feminine instincts.

In our time and culture we have seen the emergence of a feminine reaction against "The Fathers," a reaction against the collective masculine authority position. And we have seen an Amazon-like assertion of women that may be the strongest yet to have appeared in history. The collective masculine authority has devalued femininity in such a way that it can hardly function as a responsible and related spirit. Rather, it has been one-sided and irrational in its rigid view of the feminine. The collective masculine authority has functioned as a negligent father vis-à-vis the feminine. The concerted effort by women to change this cultural situation and to struggle and understand the meaning of their existence as feminine has been one of the greatest consciousness-raising events for both men and women. Yet there has been a tendency to identify with and imitate the masculine. This denies the differences between men and women. When women hope to achieve the victories of men by being like them, the uniqueness of the feminine is subtly undervalued, for there is an underlying assumption that the masculine is more powerful. This sort of reaction on the part of women is understandable since the feminine realm has been devalued in our culture. Yet, ultimately, is not the real challenge to learn to value what is uniquely feminine?

Rilke, speaking as early as 1904, described this challenge vividly in *Letters to a Young Poet:*

The girl and the woman, in their new, their own unfolding, will but in passing be imitators of masculine ways, good and bad, and repeaters of masculine professions. After the uncertainty of such transitions it will become apparent that women were only going through the profusion and the vicissitude of those (often ridiculous) disguises in order to cleanse their own most characteristic nature of the distorting influences of the other sex. Women, in whom life lingers and dwells more immediately, more fruitfully and more confidently, must surely have become fundamentally riper people, more human people, than easygoing man, who is not pulled down below the surface of life by the weight of any fruit of his body, and who, presumptuous and hasty, undervalues what he thinks he loves. This humanity of woman, borne its full time in suffering and humiliation, will come to light when she will have stripped off the conventions of mere femininity in the mutations of her outward status, and those men who do not yet feel it approaching today will be surprised and struck by it. Some day...some day there will be girls and women whose name will no longer signify merely an opposite of the masculine, but something in itself, something that makes one think, not of any complement and limit, but only of life and existence: the feminine human being.[2]

As I see it, the Amazonic reaction against the irresponsible and uncommitted father, whether manifested culturally or personally, may be a necessary phase developmentally, both on the cultural and personal levels. But, like Rilke, I think it is only a step on the way in the process of feminine development. In this chapter, I plan to explore some of the modes of existence the Amazonic reaction may take vis-à-vis the negligent father, i.e., the "Amazonic armors" which protect one from the irresponsible father, and whether there is a possible transformation beyond the reactive aspect towards the genuine and actively feminine. Once again I would like to stress that these are not intended to be "types" or categories into which any woman might neatly fit.[3] They are intended to be phenomenological descriptions of some of the different modes of behavior that might appear in a woman's life as a result of a reaction to a negligent father.

1. THE SUPER STAR

Perhaps one of the most frequent ways of reacting to an irresponsible father is to do what the father did not do in the areas of work and achievement. The sense of identity and relation to work which was not provided by the father is then achieved by the daughter herself. But the tendency to compensate for the lack in the father often leads to over-work and over-achievement by the daughter, the now-familiar workaholic pattern. Frequently the woman is left dry, cut off from her feelings and instinctive sources. This often results in depression and loss of meaning, since ultimately the identification with work alone is not enough.

Sylvia Plath's *The Bell Jar* reveals this type of existence along with its detrimental aspects. Esther Greenwood, the protagonist who is modelled on Sylvia Plath's own experiences, has been an all-A student, conquering physics even though she hates it, forcing herself to succeed regardless of how she feels. We meet her at the time when she has won, via a writing contest, a special month-long position at full salary on a prominent New York fashion magazine. The magazine has put up Esther and the other winners at a special hotel for women called "The Amazon"—a hotel mostly inhabited by rich girls. Esther herself comes from a poor background, since her father died when she was nine; and although she knows she is supposed to be having the time of her life, enjoying such success, the fact is that she is bored and depressed. Listen to her reflect:

> Look what can happen in this country, they'd say. A girl lives in some out of the way town for nineteen years, so poor she can't afford a magazine, and then she gets a scholarship to college and wins a prize here and a prize there and ends up steering New York like her own private car. Only I wasn't steering anything, not even myself. I just bumped from my hotel to work and to parties and from parties to my hotel and back to work like a numb trolleybus. I guess I should have been excited the way most of the other girls were, but I couldn't get myself to react. I felt very still and very empty, the way the eye of a tornado must feel, moving dully along in the middle of the surrounding hullabaloo.[4]

Beneath all of Esther's achievement is a deep-seated depression. No matter what she does and achieves, ultimately

65

it gives her life no meaning. To survive in this situation she develops a cynical humor which wittily objectifies and caricatures everyone whom she meets. In the same way that her cynical humor is a defense against her feeling, so is her relationship with men pervaded by a spectator-like detachment. Her relations to men are not personal but objectified— one always feels a snicker intruding. For example, she collects men with interesting names. But behind this cold attitude is the fear of rejection. As she says, "If you expect nothing from somebody, you are never disappointed."[5] Basically, Esther's experience with men has been abandonment— first via the death of her father and then through a series of impersonal relationships. Her primary perception of men is as "Women Haters." She says:

> I began to see why women-haters could make such fools of women. Women-haters were like gods: invulnerable and chock full of power. They descended, and then they disappeared. You could never catch one.[6]

Like her father who abandoned her through death, the women haters are totally unpredictable and undependable.

When Esther returns to her small home town after her month in New York, she is faced with a long summer and nothing to do, since for once she has failed to achieve. Her application to a writing course was rejected. Her depression and inertia increase since now she has nothing to do. At first she tries to avoid the gap in her life by sleep. But then finally sleep abandons her too and she is condemned to insomnia and suicidal fantasies. The only way out of her dilemma is to try to kill herself, but the attempt is unsuccessful. Without the support of a father and with a bitter martyr mother, the impersonality of her life and relationships mount until finally she feels shut off under the rarified air of a "bell jar." As she says, "To the person in the bell jar, blank and stopped as a dead baby, the world itself is the bad dream."[7]

Sent to a clinic, Esther luckily is assigned to a warm and understanding woman therapist. In the therapeutic relationship she finally finds from another woman what she has never received from father or mother—tenderness coupled with understanding. And, finally, through this relationship Esther finds the acceptance, strength, and courage to face the world again, not with absolute certainty, but as she says with "questionmarks"—questionmarks which, although they do not provide absolute control and omnipotence, do bring her the possibility of life and meaning.

In this particular pattern there is a father who has not functioned as a father due to his early death and a mother who has taken a masculine-like Amazonic position of work and martyrdom. Hence the only masculine influence has come through a mother who has denied all feeling. Her mother has not even mourned the death of Esther's father. Neither has Esther wept and mourned him, although eventually she does go in search of her father's grave and howls her loss into the cold salt rain. It is after this that she makes her suicidal attempt—a terrible solution, and yet it is that which brings her to the clinic where she finally finds help. Nowhere before has Esther found acceptance just to be herself. Her way of surviving was to develop her masculine side and to reap her identity from achievement. But her feminine feeling for herself and others was neglected, and so she was cut off from her very meaning and being as a woman.

Quite often when there is an absent father and the mother takes on a masculine role, the daughter lacks not only a genuine masculine model, but she also has no model of femininity from the mother. This was the plight of Esther. As in this case, I wonder if the initial help most often comes from another woman who has integrated the masculine and feminine principles in herself. When the concrete experience with the father is missing, it seems likely that a bridge provided by a woman's wisdom would be most accessible.

What really needs integrating here is the feminine principle, since that has been left undeveloped. Of course, the overcompensation in the area of work and achievement also leaves out the spiritual aspect of the masculine as well. But to connect with that, first must come a return to feminine feeling and instinct. It is not that work and achievement are unimportant, but for true fulfillment they must come out of one's total center and not out of a cut-off portion of oneself. By reconnecting with the feminine, work can rest in its own proper ground. The contemporary women's movement has gone through a process rather like Esther's journey. Seeing that men have failed to respect their capabilities, unique value, and potentiality, many women understandably react by asserting themselves and rejecting men. Yet their under-lying model for personal expression has frequently been masculine so that often they appear to be mere imitations of the male. The crucial issue is to realize the value of recon-necting with the feminine, to understand what is essential to being woman and to value that. This is not a way of avoiding the work of actualizing the feminine potential, but rather entails connecting with the feminine roots which ground that potential so that it can be brought forth in its own unique way.

Super stars frequently come into analysis, exhausted from work and in search of relationship. Quite often they feel men are afraid of them because they have achieved so much and are so competent. Also they often compensate for weak fathers who were unable to achieve themselves. I suspect these women are often made into sons by fathers wishing to live vicariously their own unactualized potentialities.

One woman who followed this pattern had, in the course of analysis, a dream in which she bought a very heavy winter coat from an academic dean who had cheated her. The coat was her Amazon armor. In the dream a woman analyst told her to drop the coat and risk to fly. She realized that so many of her achievements were compensations for relationship and felt cheated by having to work all the time, rather than feeling free to play and to be—a mode which was denied her as a child. Another successful professional woman with whom I worked had many dreams in which she shouted in rage at weak, impotent men who held some control over her, as her father had done out of his own ineffectiveness and unconscious projections. She too was an over-achiever, com-pensating for a depressed and ineffectual father and a mother who was unconsciously ambitious but not achieving herself. Later this woman had many dreams of playful men and of children and finally uncovered her own lighter side and was able to express it with others.

2. THE DUTIFUL DAUGHTER

Another example of Amazon reaction is shown by Ingmar Bergman in his film *Face to Face*. Jenny, the main character of the film, is a professional woman, a psychiatrist who is disciplined, capable, responsible, and well-adjusted. She is married to a talented colleague, has a daughter, and her life seems to be going along a comfortable and predictably successful course. Yet, unexpectedly, she has a breakdown and finds herself in a hospital after an attempted suicide. The film focuses on Jenny's encounter with a series of hallucinations and dreams which take her back to her past and into a realm which her rational adaptation had hitherto denied.

At the beginning of the film, Jenny is challenged by one of her woman patients who accuses her of being unable to love, unable to show vulnerability, and of resorting to her psychiatrist persona as a means of power and control. This confrontation sets the scene for the further series of confrontations from Jenny's unconscious. At the time when this happens, Jenny is staying for two months with her grandparents since her husband and daughter are away. Back in the place where she grew up, memories begin to arise and, together with her over-worked and exhausted state, the memories and dreams begin to intrude upon her well-organized life. The main image which appears over and over again is that of a frightening old woman dressed in black or grey, with one eye gouged out, the socket staring and empty. This image symbolizes the blind and staring negative duty complex that has taken rule over Jenny's life. As a child Jenny was very close and cuddly with her father, who was very kind but an alcoholic. Her mother and grandmother criticized and looked down on her father and eventually Jenny was embarrassed by her father's hugs and kisses. And then suddenly her parents were killed in a plane crash. Jenny went to live with her grandmother who ruled with an iron discipline—no crying, no softness, no weakness, no laziness, no pleasure. Only duty, discipline, and control were valued. Jenny buckled under in her ego adaptation to become first the good daughter and later the conscientious, responsible, reliable adult. She was dutiful to this projection coming from her grandmother, but underneath lay the inhibited, paralyzed child.

As her hallucinations take their course, Jenny finds herself confronted by the people in her psyche whom she had carefully tucked away. And in the final hallucination, she finds herself in a red dress, lying in her own coffin, dead yet alive. She tries to struggle out and her red dress protrudes. But a clergyman takes a pair of her grandmother's scissors and carefully cuts the dress so that nothing will show and he can close the lid, putting Jenny and her red dress out of the picture. In protest, Jenny sets fire to the coffin; there is a momentary glimpse of the red dress and of someone inside struggling, and then the whole thing goes up in flames.

Here is an image of all the feeling and passion which Jenny has locked up inside, tucked away in a coffin, trying to struggle out and to live. The clergyman with the grand-mother's scissors is a symbol for the old forces of duty, control, and properness which try to cut off Jenny's feeling and passion, symbolized by the red dress. But the result is one huge flame, a passionate fire not to be suppressed.

It is after this hallucination that Jenny finally emerges from her breakdown and attempted suicide with some new insights. She recognizes that her attempts to control have stifled her life. Now she realizes that with her inability to let go, the joy went out of everything, even the joy of her own daughter, whom she has been unable to love. At the end, as with Esther in the previous example, we are left with questionmarks. The breakdown is over; more insight and new life have emerged. But Jenny still stands at a threshold of life into which she must move to be open to herself and others. Bergman's ending of the screenplay seems hopeful to me, for when Jenny returns to her grandmother's house, she realizes that her grandmother is suffering and old and that "in some way Grandma has become smaller, not very much, but quite noticeably."[8] Symbolically, this suggests that the negative influence coming from the grandmother has noticeably diminished. And suddenly Jenny feels genuine affection for her. At the end of the screenplay Jenny again meets the sarcastic old woman with the gouged-out eye. But this time she befriends her, perhaps with the understanding and compassion needed to transform the sarcastic, negative figure within.

The major issue for women who have fallen into the "dutiful daughter" pattern is to see that the duty pattern has been imposed on them by someone else. It is important for such women to see that this image has been projected upon them and is not really their own. While the dutiful daughter image gives the illusion of goodness and virtue, it also denies the shadow and all its life and creativity. It denies a large portion of the personality and ultimately the link to the Self. No wonder there is often exhaustion, dryness, and lack of meaning. Hence this type of woman tends to live behind a persona modelled in an image that is really not her own, an image that is duty-bound and usually to a very strict authoritarian structure. Historically, an example of this can be found in many nuns, since they were trained to be dutiful daughters, obedient to a Mother Superior who in turn is obedient to a strict authoritarian system. This system demanded that their bodies be concealed. The nun was traditionally dressed in clothing which functioned as armor to hide her femininity and to protect her from men and the temptations of the world. As one nun expressed it to me, "I now have the task of de-armoring the Amazon." To de-armor or to shed the persona involves being open and showing one's darker and weaker sides, the sides that have been suppressed or repressed by obedience to the strong, rigid authority. This entails giving up the controls established by that obedience, and it involves a certain danger, for the previously non-allowed side is undeveloped and primitive. But if this

71

opening is not done consciously, it may happen by surprise, as in the case of Jenny's nervous breakdown.

The dutiful daughter usually finds herself in the service of others to the neglect of her own creative and/or relational possibilities. One dutiful daughter I know had a father who discouraged her from following him in his profession. He felt women could be assistants, but not doctors or lawyers or professors, etc. So the daughter went only so far in her education and then quit. But she longed to become a "real" professional. She also had a secret fantasy in which she entered a convent and ultimately was required to sacrifice her journals and have her hair cut off. This fantasy, in my view, corresponded to the sacrifices her father required her to make if she was to receive his love; a sacrifice of her creative energy. Then she had a dream. She was married to a king and became pregnant with her own baby. But the king (for her a symbol of the father) didn't want her to give birth because the new baby might upset the lineage. So he put her in prison. To escape from prison she killed a nun and then put on the nun's robes so she wouldn't be recognized. In some ways, this woman was hidden in a nun's dress, because her creative potentialities were hidden. As a student she felt she had to please her teachers, again enacting the dutiful daughter. Yet she also knew she would have to leave them finally to go on her own. And so she lived under a constant burden of guilt—guilt towards them because she knew she'd have to leave them and go out on her own as she needed to leave her father's projections upon her. She had guilt towards herself because she wasn't as yet leaving. So far the only escape was to go into seclusion, i.e., the nun's clothes. But after a lot of work on herself, she began to have dreams of winning. In one dream a pregnant woman won the Kentucky Derby. For her this dream was an image acknowledging her own creative potentiality.

3. THE MARTYR

Petrification into the martyr mode is another form of Amazon armor and entails a lifestyle which is bound by limitation and passive resentment often masked by a long-suffering face. Fellini's film *Juliet of the Spirits* shows the struggles of this type of woman. Juliet, who is called "little sad face," is in a conventional marriage without any life. Her husband is tired, emotionally distant, and unfaithful to her, although Juliet tries to ignore these facts and appear the contented wife. The first shock of truth about her life comes when she goes to a seance and is told by the spirits, "No one needs you; you're nothing to no one." She tries to ignore this message, but childhood memories begin to descend upon her. There are the beautiful images she had as a child, but also the memories of her mother and father—a coldly elegant, indifferent mother and a fascist-type father, both of whom sent her to a parochial school where she played the part of a martyr in the school play. As the image of herself as a martyr to be burned returns, Juliet remembers the protest of her grandfather, a lively, unconventional man who eventually ran off with a circus bareback rider. In adult life, Juliet still plays the part of the martyred saint in her marriage, keeping silent, never confronting her husband, suppressing both anger and joy and, along with that, her sexuality.

The crisis comes when Juliet finds out for certain that her husband is having an affair with another woman. Dreams, visions, and fantasies occur with rapid force. A major figure in her dreams and visions is a sexy naked woman, quite similar to the bareback rider her grandfather loved. Synchronistically, she meets her next door neighbor, Suzy, a free, sensual woman reveling in a Dionysian lifestyle. Suzy entices Juliet into the world of play and fun. But although she goes to one of Suzy's parties and begins to enter this world of sensuality, the image of the martyr intrudes and so she leaves. Juliet's conscious ego-adaptation continues to disintegrate, however, and more images from the unconscious invade her life—starving Turkish invaders; emaciated, exhausted horses; and a martyr who becomes a whore. In the meantime, Juliet goes to a psychodrama therapist who tells her she identifies too much with her problems (a typical martyr syndrome) and that she needs to be spontaneous and relax. As Juliet realizes she is afraid of being happy and that her marriage is really a prison, her jealous, aggressive, and revengeful feelings begin to emerge. She weeps and is tempted with suicide. But with these negative feelings come many different possibilities. Along with anger comes assertion, and in an imaginative fantasy, Juliet tells her huge, cold, distant mother that she frightens her no longer. As she does this, a door opens and Juliet frees the martyred child, whereupon the rejecting mother and all the tortured figures disappear and her grandfather enters and welcomes the child. With the martyr bondage now broken and the child spirit allowed to be, Juliet is free to leave the prison of her home, breathe the fresh air, and be open to what comes.

Like many women caught in the martyr structure, Juliet has been possessive in her marriage but has lived in the shadow of her husband. Due to her martyr adaptation, she is caught by the limitation of collective values which inhibit her individuality and her unique feminine beauty. Fellini, writing about this film, says its intention "is to restore to the woman her true independence, her indisputable and inalienable dignity. A free man, I mean, cannot do without a free woman. The wife must not be the Madonna, nor an instrument of pleasure, and least of all a servant."[9]

A chief feature of the martyr lifestyle is to be the hardworking servant, either as wife or mother or both. The mother-martyr pattern emerges often when the daughter has continually heard her mother criticize and look down upon her father as weak and negligent. If the father has not contested this effectively, the daughter quite often picks up the mother's attitude, either consciously or unconsciously. Jung gives many examples of this in his word association experiment studies, e.g., the case of the sixteen-year-old daughter who had the same reactions toward men as did her mother, though without the same experiences.[10] When the daughter later marries, she often chooses a weak and passive man and passes the same attitude down to her own daughter, continuing the pattern. This type of woman falls into the mother role in relation to her husband, who is then reduced to the status of son. Alexander Lowen has described this pattern in his book *Love and Orgasm* and says that self-denial is a chief feature of this personality structure—hence the martyrdom. He points out that the mother-martyr role has a passive-submissive masochistic aspect which covers up a feeling of superiority, hostility, and contempt of the male. She dominates him through her martyrdom and puts him in the inferior position of son. She can do this either through too much nurturing and food-giving (the "Jewish mother") and/or through being the disciplinarian for the children. Especially in this latter case, the father makes none of the important decisions concerning family life even though he may be a successful breadwinner. Along with the martyrdom, according to Lowen, often goes an asexual approach to the husband, which is emasculating.[11]

Common to this pattern is the stoic self-denial which appears frequently in the areas of sexuality and creativity. In my view, this stems from a fear of the Dionysian, a fear of letting oneself go out of control, a fear of the irrational and correlatively of the transrational, i.e., those experiences which transcend ego-control, as for example love, hope, and beauty. The fear closes this type of woman off from the joy and exuberance of life and from her own creativity and special vision. The frequent cases of women in their thirties suddenly plunging into extramarital affairs and promiscuity may be an unconscious attempt to break away from this self-imposed martyrdom. But since it usually remains unconscious, perhaps even lived out in the shadow mode of the misfit, transformation is not achieved. Such a woman needs to consciously let herself into the flow of experience which includes both sexuality and creative impulses, recognizing, accepting, and forming them. And, as in the case of Juliet, it may be anger and rage which brings about this loosening. The martyr needs to get angry at her own self-denial and to recognize that the shadow side of her strong, virtuous self-denial is the "waif," the misfit who feels herself to be a rejected victim and wants to be pitied. The martyrdom is really a kind of defense reaction against the flow of experience; she wants to be acknowledged and pitied for her self-denial, playing upon the guilt feelings of those around her.

Many martyred women come into analysis, and in some ways I feel there is an inherent martyrdom that comes out of submitting to our patriarchal culture. While this has aspects of a passive puella pattern, what I find here is a hard, powerful edge that is castrating to the woman herself and to those others in her life. One typical example is a married woman whose teenage children took drugs and got into trouble with the police. She had grown up in a rich aristocratic family, and her father was patriarchal, domineering, and held control over the financial resources. In such cases the father is often absent emotionally, providing no model of independence for the daughter. Her husband was like her own father; absent as an emotional force in the family, yet financially controlling. On the one side this woman was extremely intelligent and fought to develop herself against the domineering opposition of her husband. On the other side she felt over-burdened with too many responsibilities and her frequent reaction was to become hysterical, threaten suicide, say she couldn't go on anymore. Her aggression was going overtly toward herself but covertly towards her children and her husband. While her husband seemed strong and threatening, he also felt weak and threatened. The children seemed to be acting out all the conflicts in the family: one got arrested, one became a good student, one left home. This woman finally had to assert herself and leave her marriage in which she felt the victim. Once she took active responsibility for her own power, rather than using it defensively against herself and others, she was able to actualize her creative energies.

4. THE WARRIOR QUEEN

Still another mode of reaction to the irresponsible and weak father is to become a strong and determined fighter. In this case the daughter opposes all the irrationality that was experienced as degenerate in the father and fights against him. C.S. Lewis describes this type of woman in his novel *Till We Have Faces*, which is his version of the Psyche-Amor myth retold from the perspective of one of the jealous sisters. In the novel the father is a destructively brutal king who sacrifices his youngest daughter, Psyche, to the goddess Aphrodite in order to appease his subjects who have complained that Psyche is responsible for the famine and plague which have been tormenting the land. That he sacrifices her is a reflection of his general lack of spirit. His main interests are in parties, hunting game, acquiring money, and lusting for new acquisitions. He spends no time with his daughters and in fact is disgusted with them for not being sons. When he is involved with them, it is in the form of terrible rages, abusing them by calling one a whore (a daughter who follows the puella pattern) and the other ugly. The "ugly one," Orual, is the oldest. At Psyche's birth, Orual took over the mother role since Psyche's mother died, and so she regarded Psyche as her child, loving her with a fierce mother-love. When the father sacrificed Psyche, Orual lost her most valued possession, her beloved Psyche.

Orual hates her father and everything that he represents. She despises the irrational realm which she has experienced only as degenerate via her father. And she transfers her hatred to the entire realm of the gods, in whom she alternatively disbelieves but also hates for taking her beloved sister, Psyche, away from her. In her mind, the gods and her father are of one kind. She thinks as follows:

> It is, in its way, admirable, this divine skill. It was not enough for the gods to kill her [Psyche], they must make her father the murderer...Now mark yet again the cruelty of the gods. There is no escape from them into sleep or madness, for they can pursue you into them with dreams. Indeed, you are then most at their mercy. The nearest thing we have to a defense against them (but there is no real defense) is to be very wide awake and sober and hard at work, to hear no music, never to look at earth or sky, and (above all) to love no one.[12]

Here one can see clearly the building up of a negative, rigid consciousness, a rejection of feeling and life as a reaction to the destructiveness of the negative father. On the collective level, as king, he symbolizes an irresponsible relationship to the feminine, i.e., an inadequate cultural valuation of the feminine. Orual reacts to this by fighting her father. She even learns to wield a sword more powerfully than any man, and when her father dies, she takes over the throne. But her bitterness remains, for she realizes that her life is only a life of work. She is a sad and lonely queen who has chosen to lead a man's life.

Consumed even more with bitterness and hatred for the gods, Orual decides to write a testament of accusation against them. In doing so she becomes possessed with her father's own fury, and, as she writes, she is suddenly assailed with dreams and visions. In one dream, her father forces her to go into the palace basement and there to descend even further into a black hole where he confronts her, holding a mirror so that she sees clearly who she is. In the mirror Orual sees that she looks like her father. It is then that she realizes that through her reaction to her father, through her attempt to be his opposite, she has ended in the same irrational mode. Her attempt to become strong and rational only covered up an irrational rage and jealousy that was just like her father's. In this moment of recognition, she realizes that her task is not to fight the irrational, but to transform that which has become degenerate spirit (symbolized by her father's relation to life) into the holy. Recognizing that her defiance in the face of the gods was an ego attempt (just like her father's) to control and possess, she surrenders to the greater power of the gods and finally is able to love.

At one point, Orual has said to herself that her aim was "to build up more and more that strength, hard and joyless, which had come to me when I heard the god's sentence; by learning, fighting and laboring, to drive all the woman out of me."[13] In this fighter pattern, the father and often all other men are rejected and despised as weak, and the daughter feels that she alone is strong enough to do what has to be done. But the irony is that the way of strength is taken over from a masculine model and so the feminine is still devalued by this type of woman. Quite often one feels in such a woman the gritting of teeth, the do or die of strong determination. For the woman who lives out this type of existence, life becomes a chore and a series of battles to be won rather than moments to be enjoyed. Grim and somber, she stridently moves ahead, disregarding feelings and the feminine body which are hidden behind her battle shield. Instead of fighting for the genuine strength of feminine receptivity, she sees that as weak passivity. Perhaps this is the pattern that many of the more militant women take when they insist that there are no differences between men and women and when they reduce receptivity to weak passivity.

An example of this pattern can be seen in Bobbie, who came into analysis feeling trapped in a fighter role. She felt she was hard, living like a man. She wanted to be open and receptive and to be in a relationship, but she felt tight and closed. Her father, though in many ways a warm man, had given all his daughters boys' names. He had ambitious professional expectations of them and she felt she had been raised as a son rather than a daughter. So she became ambitious and competitive—a tough fighter—and she felt this had broken up her marriage and stood in the way of her relationships. She was also very tough on herself, unrelentingly critical.

During the course of analysis she began to meditate, practice Tai Chi, and to study an artform. These opened her up and gradually she felt more receptive and spontaneous with people. Then she had a series of dreams with positive feminine figures in them. One was a wise old woman who had written a book on the feminine. Another was a young girl who ran freely in fields of grass. Then she had a dream that she was lying down while another woman was stroking her clitoris. A man was lying inert by her side. She was not turned on by the woman and was also worried the man would be offended by smelling the vaginal juices. She mentioned this to the other woman who replied that he should like the smell of femininity.

This dream came at a time when she was opening up, feeling her softer side and her spontaneity. But there were still tendencies to judge herself and for a role reversal in which she felt she should please men by becoming passive, i.e., a darling doll. The dream, she felt, revealed three sides of herself. The inert man symbolized her former masculine part that had rejected the soft side of the feminine, the side that corresponded to the projection of her father and reflected the views of the patriarchal culture. The other woman she associated to a young lesbian woman—not a militant type who disliked men, but rather a woman fighting for feminine rights in a centered feminine way. The way she saw herself in the dream was as a darling doll type (her shadow side) who wanted to please men and adapt to the masculine values. Her reaction to the dream was that she wanted to relate to the other woman, a symbol of her feminine self, but her old masculine macho pattern and its darling doll opposite side were still in the way. Yet the stronger figure now was the active woman and this was the way she was beginning to feel. This is an example of a woman who was beginning to take her warrior queen strengths with her, but not via an armored defense system. Rather she was integrating them with her softer side so they could be there in a strong feminine way expressive of herself.

The Armored Amazon's Despair

What are some of the common features of the armored Amazon? Central is the desire to control. Since she tends to see the man as weak and impotent, or is reacting against his irrational use of power, she seizes the power herself. Being in control makes things seem safe and secure. But along with that control may go an overdose of responsibility, duty, and a feeling of exhaustion. The need to control is due often to a fear of the irrational so that it is eliminated as far as possible from life. But when this happens, one is then cut off from

80

spontaneity and the unexpected, and these put the zest and charm in life. Frequently such women are alienated as well from feeling and relationship, since the need to control doesn't allow things to happen. At bottom, one is alienated from the deeper roots of creativity and spirituality whenever this controlling attitude dominates. No wonder, then, that Amazonic women often eventually feel that life has become dry and meaningless. And no wonder when the spontaneous forces that have been so repressed or suppressed suddenly assert themselves and break down the existing psychic structure as they frequently do in depression, anxiety attacks, and the feeling that one can't handle things anymore.

Dominating the Amazonic attitude is an overemphasis on limitation and necessity. Kierkegaard has described this attitude as a form of despair which he calls "The Despair of Necessity." This type of despair is an alienation from the totality of the whole person and occurs when one identifies with finitude and necessity so much that one denies all possibility, including the essential possibility of the Self. And to what does this lead? According to Kierkegaard, when one sees oneself as only finite one becomes

> a number, just one man more, one more repetition...Despairing narrowness consists in the lack of primitiveness, or of the fact one has deprived oneself of one's primitiveness; it consists in having emasculated oneself, in a spiritual sense.[14]

The tendency here, Kierkegaard claims, is to become "worldly," i.e., to become so wise about how things work in the world that one adapts. Although that leads to success in the world as one learns to adapt to the demands of the world's business, it also leads to becoming an adapted imitation of others. The danger is that one forgets that the Self is a higher power, that one fears to allow the spontaneity that cannot be controlled since it may cause one to lose one's safe and established position. Like King Midas who, to secure himself completely, turned everything, including his food, into gold and starved to death, so does this attitude starve one of the vital life substance. As Kierkegaard says, the man crushed down by despair strains himself against existence. Ultimately this attitude is "the despair of willing despairingly to be oneself—defiance."[15] For at bottom one defiantly refuses possibility, refuses what is beyond the ego's power to control. Taken to the extreme, this attitude is demonic for it refuses all help from a greater power, seeing all power and strength to exist only in oneself.

The armored Amazon's stance of strength is truly desperate and super-human. Hence a breakdown of this pose of strength quite often happens—just as it happened to each of the women in the films and novels discussed. In each case there was a breakdown of the existing ego-posture of strength and a reduction to weakness and helplessness before the irrational. Jenny, Juliet, and Orual became victims of hallucinations; Esther and Jenny became subject to suicidal impulses. The crucial challenge for each, as it was for myself and for many of my clients, was to accept the weakness, depression, and inability to work and function. Frequently this means an encounter with our rage and our tears. Many women sit in my office, shaking in anger or tears. Frequently they are ashamed and humiliated by their lack of control. They "shouldn't" weep or rage, they often say, because this is a sign of inferiority. They also often feel headed for a nervous breakdown. Yet if they can accept the validity of their feelings, that acceptance can give them new humility to open themselves up to the flow of life.

Toward Transformation

Of course, the total breakdown of an Amazon armor is an extreme situation. In analysis, we hope for a conscious transformation before a breakdown occurs. How, then, is this transformation to occur? How can the woman trapped in an Amazon armor free herself?

A first step is to see the kind of armor in which she is trapped. Without this recognition, she will continue the pattern of defending herself against that which is inside. She will need to accept her shadow of weakness. Unlike the puella, whose conscious posture is weakness, the Amazon's ego-adaptation is strength and power. But underneath that shell of strength one often finds helplessness and dependence and an overpowering need that can consume those around her. The martyr masks herself as a suffering worker, but underneath falls victim to self pity and wants the pity of others. The superstar's strength is in her achievements, but when her achievements lose meaning, as they often do when they are ego devices for attention, she is likely to fall into an inability to do anything at all. The dutiful daughter's dependable obedience to work and to the demands of others may cover up an inner rebellion and desire for flight which can crack apart her ordered world, leaving herself and others subject to confusion and chaos. And the warrior queen's icy hardness may suddenly melt into an unexpected emotional attachment which could devastate both herself and the other because it is so possessively dependent.

Accepting the shadow of weakness does not mean to flip over permanently into a puella position, although this may be a necessary moment in her development. The Amazonic woman has already developed a lot of strength and power in her life and this is very valuable. The issue is rather to allow that strength to come out naturally from the center of her personality rather than be forced out from an ego adaptation. What is needed is to bring that strength to the area of which she is afraid. It is neither a weakness to be in the irrational realm nor to use it as a source of knowledge. To the contrary, it is a weakness to be unable to face this aspect of life. If the Amazon woman can learn to value her vulnerability and the uncontrollable aspects of existence, she may find a new source of strength. The creative process offers many examples of the necessity to go down into the unconscious and remain there in weakness, perhaps in depression, boredom, or anxiety, in order to bring up the "new being," the creative attitude which can change one's life. The way to this is not a way of "doing"—which is the Amazon's usual mode of action. In my experience "not doing" is the secret.

While I was revising this chapter, I found myself trapped in two terrible Amazon armors—that of the superstar and the martyr. My creative energies were blocked. I had a deadline to meet, and I felt totally exhausted. I could not write one more word. The burden seemed unbearable. And it extended beyond the chapter, for I began to feel I couldn't meet any of my other obligations either. So then I finally gave up the task of writing and went for a walk in nature and visited some friends. They suggested that I ask the *I Ching* about my Amazon armor trap and when I did, I received the hexagram, "Opposition." There was the image of my condition: two daughters who "...although they live in the same house, they belong to different men; hence their wills are not the same but are divergently directed."[16] The two daughters, as I interpreted them, were my own Amazon and puella sides caught in a stark opposition. The puella wanted to play and the Amazon needed to work. And caught between these two, I felt trapped and could do nothing. The advice I received was as follows: "If you lose your horse, do not run after it; It will come back of its own accord."[17] The *I Ching* was telling me I could not force things and that, if I did, I would only achieve the opposite of what I wanted. If one runs after a horse, he only runs farther away. Better to let it come back on its own. And this is the way it was with the creative energy for my writing. I had to wait until it came back. And somehow this image which the *I Ching* gave me released me to wait in ease.

Another aspect of transformation of the armored Amazon is freeing herself of the idea she must be like a man to have power. Many Amazon women are ruled by a reaction to an inadequate father, whether on the personal or cultural levels, or both. So it is natural that an ego identification with the masculine might compensate that which was left undeveloped by the father. The tendency here is to develop the strong heroic mode of existence. The Amazon has identified primarily with the heroic masculine, and that identification needs to be recognized and released. If the Amazon woman doesn't want to crack, she needs a softening of the armor. This softening may help her find a creative relationship to the feminine in herself and the feminine in men. This seems to be a major issue of our time as well, because the armored woman, in fighting for her rights, has most often had to do

84

this by relating to men vis-à-vis a power attack. She has had to take up a sword and fight as a man. But then, like Orual, she has sword, shield, and mask, but is left without relationship.

Perhaps since her first identification is with the masculine, her armor can be softened by a loving masculine figure. Such an image, "The Man with Heart," came up in one of my own dreams. In the dream a young man had moved, without my knowledge, into my new house and had decorated a room there. This young man loved nature, hiking, and traveling, and he had brought with him wonderfully colored hand-woven rugs from Poland and Mexico. The rug motifs were birds and flowers, and the major background color was a soft mellow rose. In this room were cozy couches and chairs, these beautiful rugs, and soft, clear lighting. He was sitting there very comfortably in his pajamas on one of the couches listening to music and reading a book. In the dream I fell deeply in love with him. When I awoke in the middle of the night, I went all through my house looking for this room and the young man. But alas, I couldn't find them. At first I was heartbroken. But then I realized that here was an image to help me find within myself that man who liked women and could create a warm, cozy, comfortable atmosphere.

Another example of a masculine image to soften a woman's armor is the great lover Casanova. In her 1975 Jung Memorial lecture in Zurich, Hilde Binswanger compared two famous lovers, Don Juan and Casanova, and said they might be looked at as two different inner masculine images. Don Juan, the lover who seduced women and then left them bitter and negative towards both men and themselves, she compared to the way the negative inner man works. Casanova, the lover who loved many women and made each feel feminine and beloved, she took to be an image of a positive inner man, one that leaves the woman feeling good about herself. With these images in mind, it seems to me the Amazon-armored woman has been fighting the Don Juan image, an image which I find similar to the "perverted old man," that inner masculine figure who dislikes women and hacks away at their self-valuation and confidence. But in the fight she has often become hardened herself. In contrast, Casanova's tender touch is sensitively related to the feminine. With him she can respond creatively and receptively out of the strong center of her own femininity.

It may be that at first this softer and gentler masculine aspect appears as a "Dummling," as a weak and ineffective fool who doesn't know how to do things. In fairy tales and in the symbolism of the Tarot cards, the dummling or fool figure stumbles around without direction, and yet in losing his footage he usually falls upon the new and unknown. And it is precisely the new and unknown that tends to be missing from the Amazon's life because it is that against which her armor protects her. This dummling or fool figure is closely connected to the feminine and the instinctual levels. In the Waite deck of the Tarot, he has a rose in one hand and a dog by his side; in fairy tales he often sits down and cries and also feeds animals who then help him to save the princess trapped on a glass mountain or in a tower. Since I have elaborated this theme in another chapter, here I want only to provide a hint in this direction—that the image of the dummling may be helpful for both the acceptance and valuation of the shadow of weakness and the creative relationship to the feminine.

In contrast to the puella whose task of transformation is to accept her strength and develop it, the Amazon's transformation involves softening, allowing the receptivity in herself to be so that it can unite with her already-developed strength in the creative expression of her feminine spirit.

CHAPTER FIVE

THE MAN WITHIN

The basic discovery about any people
is the discovery of the relationship
between its men and women.
                                    Pearl S. Buck

The father is the first experience a woman has of the masculine. In this way he provides an important model for the way she relates to man and to her own inner masculine side. I have found some recurring masculine images in the dreams of women with injured relationships to their fathers. Often appearing in the dreams and experience of the woman who tends toward the puella pattern of the eternal girl is a figure I call "The Perverted Old Man." And in the dreams and experience of the armored Amazon there arises frequently the figure of "The Angry Boy."

Since the puella woman tends to deny her own strength and power and instead falls under the powerful and authoritarian masculine, a perversion of this power takes place and she seems to become victim to a critical judge within. In contrast, the armored Amazon tends to deny her own playful side. In masculine form this side of the Amazon becomes like an angry, rebellious adolescent who needs to assert himself and break her armored control. In order to develop a better relation to the masculine within and without, a woman needs to become conscious of these figures in her psyche and how they affect her. Once she faces these figures, a new and more creative relation to the masculine can emerge.

1. THE PUELLA AND THE PERVERTED OLD MAN

Many a woman has said to me in the course of analysis: "How can I do this?...I'm no good....Everything I do is wrong....There is no hope....No one will ever love me." And having also said this to myself a time or two too many, I began to wonder what lies behind such a lack of spirit; what lies behind such a negative self-image? What keeps women so unconfident and insecure that they remain eternal girls, caught in the archetypal pattern of the puella?

Suddenly a recurrent motif sprang to mind, a common image in the dreams of many female analysands and in my own dreams as well—the image of a perverted and sadistic old man. The following dream illustrates this theme.

In the dream a sexually perverted old man is following a young, innocent girl, waiting for the moment he might grab her. The moment would be, he said, when she started to wear long dresses; that is, at the moment she would be ready to become a woman. At that moment he planned to destroy her. But the innocent young girl had a girl friend who warned her about this man so she was able to face him and confront him head on. His plan to grab her from behind foiled, the perverted old man became enraged and lunged towards the girl, but she kicked him in the crotch and sent him reeling backwards. Even madder, the old man picked up a bucket of waste water that had been used to wash strawberries and tried to throw it at her. But the girl was too quick and grabbed the bucket, throwing the water back on him. As she did so, a voice said: "This is a task in the fairy tales of four different languages."

This dream shows the connection between these two figures: the puella and the perverted old man. It also shows the moment when the puella can grow up, and it highlights the danger of that moment. For then the conscious confrontation begins and with it the possibility of dealing with this inner figure. I will return to this possibility later. But first I would like to look a bit more at these two figures, the puella and the perverted old man, to discover why and how they belong together.

Just as every Persephone has a Pluto who abducts her and pulls her underground, so in the psyche of the puella dwells a sick manifestation of the rigid authoritarian side of the masculine. He is potentially a wise old man who has become sick and nasty because he has been neglected. In my view this neglect is due to a wounded father development in which the father has not been there for his daughter in a committed and responsible way on the eros and logos levels. That is, the father has not functioned as a father.

When the father principle, which provides a sense of inner authority and spirit, is lacking or misformed, there is the opportunity for the perverted old man to enter. In my experience, whenever there is a potentiality in the psyche that is not being used, there is the chance for its perversion. The father potentiality is one that we all have within us, women and men alike. But to develop a potentiality we need experience. We need over and over again to explore and experiment, to test and try, and this is the way we grow and learn to use whatever is inside of us.

Now if the father is not concretely there for his daughter, or if he is there in a negative way in the course of her development, how is she to experience and learn about this part of herself? Most likely she will have to rely on what she hears from her mother and her relatives and on cultural impressions and on the fantasies that grow because the reality was lacking. Quite likely, if the father was not there for his daughter, neither was he there as husband for his wife. So her mother is likely to have an embittered or cynical view of men and a perverted, negative inner man, i.e., a negative relation to the masculinity in herself. It is not surprising, then, that the daughter may grow up with the same negative view of father and men, and with a distorted relation to masculinity within. With imagination working at full capacity on the negative, a Bluebeard view of man can easily emerge. This can happen inwardly or on the cultural level, too. Suppose a woman grew up in Nazi Germany—an extreme example to be sure but one where the fascist brute ruled. What image of father and spirit could she have then? Or even in America where so often the men remain boys and where there is so much divorce and lack of commitment—so much of the transitory.

When the father image is damaged, so is the image of men. The woman tends to experience men negatively and with distrust. But the manner in which the distorted view of father and men is manifested differs for the puella and the Amazon. The Amazon tends to see men as weak and inferior, as powerless. It is she who is the strong and powerful one; it is she who is independent. Men are of little or no consequence in her world. In contrast, the puella gives up her power to men. She is the dependent one, a victim at the mercy of the powerful male. He calls the shots, while she complies either willingly or unwillingly. It is not hard to see how a sadism-masochism syndrome occurs. Having given all her power to the man, there is little left for herself, and her self-confidence and esteem are very low. Of course, in the unconscious is quite likely a huge inflation—a high and unrealistic image of herself. She may feel like the sensitive princess who can't sleep on the pea because she is too good for anything inferior. But consciously she may feel like Cinderella who is neglected and abused and relegated to the dirt and ashes. One woman had a dream which illustrates this clearly. Her manfriend was praising a very confident woman who was narcissisti-cally viewing herself while the dreamer was working in the pantry, deboning chickens. Finally the dreamer couldn't take it any longer and she flew into a rage, telling the other woman how inflated she was. And that was what she needed to do in reality—to recognize the unconscious, inflated, narcissistic attitude that enslaved her to the inferior view she had of herself.

In the puella's attitude toward herself one often can hear a snide and cynical voice telling her she is no good, that she will never accomplish anything, and neither is she worthy of love. When she believes this voice, a vicious circle ensues which perpetuates this negative view of herself as weak and worthless. She does indeed often "fail" in the outer world, but that is because she has given over all her power to this sadistic inner man who both tells her she will fail but also feeds her inflation.

This operates in the four different puella lifestyles: the "darling doll" who lives out her male partner's projections; the "girl of glass" who lives in a fantasy world unable to face reality; the "high flyer" who flies amorously and uncommittedly from man to man; and the "misfit" who is the bad girl and an outcast to society. At bottom, a lack of self-confidence, listening to the brute within, drives all these women into lives that are unfulfilled. One of my analysands had a dream that on the way to a baby or a wedding shower she parked in a dead end where an old man tried to steal her car. When she saw him, he slit all the tires so she couldn't drive it. No wonder, then, that she was unable to move, to put into reality and bring to birth the full extent of her creative potential, which was quite high indeed.

It is often said against women that they have never proven themselves. "Where are the women in history who have created?", one constantly hears. But if indeed the development I have described is somewhat typical, then it would seem to me to be no surprise. The puella must deal with the perverted old man within who hacks away at her potential before she is able to create and actualize her achievements in the world.

One way the perverted old man has functioned culturally, I believe, is to impose a masculine view of creativity upon women, a tyranny of logic and reason. If she follows this rule, then she must create as a man and not from her inner feminine center. No wonder there have been so few women who have "made it": they are denied their own way of creating. And, in addition to imposing masculine standards and judgments on women's creativity, the perverted old man has been functioning culturally by making them feel guilty if

91

they take time for themselves to create. Anaïs Nin, who lived much of her life as a puella and who was a puer's daughter but who managed to create and contribute to the world, expressed the situation very clearly. She says:

> There is also an extra problem that women have about writing that men don't and that is guilt. Somehow woman has associated the activity of creating, the creative will, with a masculine concept and has had the fear that this activity was an aggressive act. Because culture didn't demand achievement of a woman. It demanded it of the man. So the man had no guilt for locking himself up and writing a novel and not paying attention to his family for three months. But women had been almost inbred with the sense that their personal life was their first major duty, and that their writing had to do with self-expression. She confused that with subjectivity and narcissism, whereas we never spoke of a man writer as a narcissist.[1]

It is not that I am excusing or justifying the lack of creativity of women on these grounds. Not at all, for that would be to fall into the pattern of the puella, the victim, the helpless girl who is at the mercy of those mean old men. But it is necessary in my experience to understand the development of a life pattern in order to be able to change it. Usually there is both an outer and inner manifestation in a destructive life pattern, and once seen, it needs to be dealt with on both levels. In the area of creativity, it is most important for women to see how this perverted masculine figure has functioned both outwardly on the cultural level and inwardly in the psyche.

Besides creativity, sexuality and relatedness are other areas where the sadistic-masochistic pattern takes hold. In the dream mentioned above, the old man is perverted sexually and the girl is young and innocent. Sadistically, he wants to destroy her. It is as though these two belong together—innocence and perversion. Consider the following example. One woman with whom I worked in analysis and who did not have a father to whom she could relate kept looking for the father in every man she met. In the early stages of her life she was cut off from sexuality altogether, for to go to bed with one's father is forbidden. But then the shadow soon caught up with her and from sexual naïvete she flipped over into sexual promiscuity, unable to say "no" to men's demands, even if it went against her feelings. Most of the men with whom she became involved she liked very much indeed, yet she was really seeking the father. She settled for a sexual partner instead since via sex she could have the man. The men also tended to be unavailable since they were usually married, and so the lack of commitment which she experienced with her father was repeated in these situations. Because she was not really acting out of the center of her feminine eros but rather out of the need for love and commitment which her father had never given her, there was a kind of self-betrayal involved in all of these relationships as well as a betrayal of the men. Deep down she didn't trust them, otherwise she would have been able to tell them how she really felt. The way the perverted old man functioned in her was to tell her that the only way she could have a relationship was by putting her body on the market, which then undermined her confidence even more. And he also led her into relationships with men who were really unattainable. And so in her sexual "freedom" she remained locked up and as closed off from relationship and eros as she had been in her previous naïvete. But the perverted man was able to control her and keep her out of a meaningful relationship only because she gave him the power through her innocence and lack of feminine assertion, through the fact that she remained passive and dependent, enacting the girl rather than the self-confident woman.

This pattern is not so uncommon. On the outer level one need only to look at the high incidence of child abuse. Women who as young girls have been subjected to sexual abuse or even rape by older men have experienced this perversion on the outer level in a most severe way. As a result their self-confidence has usually been severely damaged, and if one looks deep within one can find the perverted old man, a torturous, negative animus continuing that abuse. Another example on the social level is the prostitute. Studies have shown that frequently she has been brutally rejected by the father and that she re-enacts that rejection and the hatred that goes with it by selling herself to men. But even in the seemingly happy housewife or the young swinger one frequently finds this pattern operating underneath.

The film *Last Tango in Paris* shows this integral relation of sadistic old man–masochistic young woman in extremity. And it shows the danger for the man as well as for the woman. As the film begins, a broken-down and depressed older man accidentally meets a lively young woman when they both answer an advertisement for an apartment. Their relationship begins on a sexual level immediately and is extremely impersonal—impersonal to the extent that the man says they are there for sex alone with no questions to be asked: they are not even to know each other's name. At first the girl wants to know about him, but finally accedes to his demand and is drawn to meet him on whatever terms he sets. What starts for her as a lark and casual encounter becomes a compulsive addiction through which she allows herself to be subjected to a variety of humiliating and debasing sexual acts. One might expect this pattern to continue indefinitely and yet the table turns. At some point along the way the man begins to fall in love with her and wants a more personal relationship. But as soon as that happens, it is the girl who begins to insist upon impersonality. Now it is she who rejects and gains control. Finally, when he pursues the personal relationship and wants to know her name, she refuses in fright and in hysterical defense shoots him to death, saying:

> I don't know who he is. He followed me on the street. He tried to rape me. He's a madman. I don't know his name. I don't know his name. I don't know who he is. He's a madman. I don't know his name.[2]

In the end she tries to justify herself through her innocence and lack of knowledge, i.e., through not knowing his name.

94

This film dramatizes to the extreme the interaction between sadistic man and masochistic girl. But perhaps even more important, it shows the other side of the picture not so often seen—that the girl, too, is sadistic, for it is she who finally kills the man and rejects the personal relationship. The other side of her submission to men is her negative feeling of distrust, even hatred toward them. Alexander Lowen in his book *Love and Orgasm* has described this dependent daughter pattern from a different perspective. He says that such a woman functions as a psychological prostitute who, having been rejected, is in great need of love. And so to get the love, she will do anything. But the enormity of this need devours the man with whom she is involved, for no matter how much the man gives her, it can never be enough. Since her need is insatiable, the lovers ultimately fail and feel guilty. In contempt she spits them out as worthless.[3]

While this is an extreme, I think there is usually an element entailed in most puella-perverted old man patterns. In the dream I first mentioned, the innocent girl must confront the perverted man. In doing so, she must pay attention to him consciously and not act as though he wasn't there, as she has in her previous innocence. It is this conscious recognition of him that allows her finally to assert herself and thereby overcome his cynical, threatening control. Throwing the waste water from the strawberries back on him is her feminine assertion, her refusal to be doused with the wastes of failed love, and an affirmation of the power of her own love. But first she has to confront this figure; i.e., to get to know him and name him. The tragedy in *Last Tango in Paris* happens when the young girl is afraid to really meet the old man, when she is afraid to know who he is, to identify him and to know his name. Conversely, in the dream as in the fairytale "Rumpelstiltskin," it is precisely knowing the name and identifying the perverted figure that prevents the tragedy and keeps the girl out of that perverted figure's clutch.

But how does this naming and identifying the figure happen? One way is through our dreams, which reveal the cast of characters within us and the dynamics operating between them. Another is understanding our projections on other people, our fantasies of how we would like them to be. Fairy tales, myths, literature, and film provide other oppor- tunities to see ourselves in the various characters and interactive patterns they reveal. Still another way is via active imagination, i.e., an active dialogue with the inner figure to find out who he is and why he is there and is acting in that way. One analysand told me about an active imagina- tion in which she conversed with a perverted old man figure who had appeared in several of her dreams. When she asked him why he was so mean and nasty, he said to her: "Little girl, you bug me with your innocent self-righteousness. You act the poor defenseless victim. You neglect me and then blame me, but I need some attention too, and that is why I'm bothering you. Try to understand me, understand why I'm so frustrated. That's why I'm nasty to you." What this figure seemed to be trying to tell her was that he was perverted because she continually ignored him and acted as though he wasn't there. And as soon as she started to pay attention to him, to talk to him and befriend him, he began to change.

So, forgetting and neglecting the perverted old man keeps the puella in her position of helplessness and passivity. On the psychological level how might this figure be neglected? One mode of neglect is not to acknowledge his existence at all. Consider, for example, the attitude of idealistic and inflated optimism that acknowledges no limits and boundaries what- soever, the high flying attitude that wants to believe all things are possible and that refuses to acknowledge the power of the demonic and shadow aspects of existence. Impatience is an example of the high flyer's neglect, it ignores the limits of time, flying into the future rather than doing what is required in the present. The darling doll is likely to fall into this trap of being unable to acknowledge her own dark side because of the overly idealistic projections her father and lovers put upon her. The flip side of this is to

96

identify, as the misfit does, with the shadow side in an attitude of rebellion which doesn't confront the perverted old man figure because it is too identified with it. Extreme indulgence in drugs, alcohol, and sex are examples of this because the natural limits of the body and the emotional life are not accepted. And the girl of glass neglects the perverted old man by retreating into her fantasy world.

The perverted old man might also be neglected by trying to run away from him. One of my analysands was pursued in a dream by a threatening older man and was trying to outrun him. When they reached a fence, she turned and kicked him in the leg, whereupon he tripped and fell into a hole that had a coffin-like box in it. She tried to bury him, but didn't finish the job and soon he was behind her again, telling her she couldn't fly away. But fly away she did and, as she flew, she was sucked by the air into a vacuum in the sky. In this case the perverted old man was consciously experienced via a frequently recurring cynical and self-critical attitude that told her she wouldn't succeed and which tormented her with feelings of guilt about her "badness." It kept her from pursuing her educational development for a number of years, and then when she finally and courageously took the risk of school, it told her she wouldn't succeed. At the time of the dream, she had started the process of confronting this inner figure, but had not yet followed through totally, and so was also still trying to run away. The vacuum in the sky into which she was drawn symbolized an empty space in herself, a feeling of depression and guilt for not having actualized her own potentialities but instead projecting her creativity onto her boyfriends. In the course of analysis, as she began to face this inner cynicism and stand her ground against it, she felt less and less a victim of circumstances and assumed responsibility for her decisions. For example, she stood behind her decision to develop herself professionally, and when the cynical, vicious voices shouted "You don't deserve to succeed," she shouted back more loudly that they were wrong, that she could reach the goals she set. And as she did so, new aspects of the world opened up for her.

One of the reasons to run away from such a figure is that it can become very devilish. The devil, after all, is the rejected and neglected one, but also the proud and vain one. And these two—rejection and pride—usually alternate in the psyche. In my own experience, when I felt rejected I tended to react by saying to myself, "Well, then, I will go away to some place where I am really valued...." But that implies of course that the rejection is not faced with conscious assertion of one's self-worth and that there is a compensation on the fantasy level that one is great indeed and those dolts who rejected were too stupid to see it. But there is also the fear that the rejecting ones were really right.

Facing the perverted old man means facing this complex of rejection-inflation. It means facing one's identification with the devil, that powerful, powerless pride that says "I cannot do it," assuming that one has all the power in oneself to decide what one can or cannot do. This attitude leaves nothing to the higher powers beyond the ego, the inner resources of healing, although one veils all that in the appearance of girlish impotence. Facing the perverted old man means risking a fight with this figure—a fight that might lead to a new-found strength, as it did for the girl in the dream who threw back the dirty water and was given confirmation that this was an acknowledged task. Facing the perverted old man also means facing the possibility that in the perversion lies some hidden possibility. The devil is after all a fallen angel, a high being whose possibility has somehow gone wrong through a distorted attitude.

The following active imagination, done by a young woman early in the course of her analysis, provides an image for finding possible value which is hidden by the perversion:

At the water's edge I stepped aboard a raft drawn by a giant swan. Gliding over the sea, we passed a large and beautiful lotus blossom and then the swan dove underwater to the entrance of a cave. There a witch met me and led me through some caverns past a wild boar and into a round room where she bade me dance with a giant cockroach. At first the three of us danced together, and then the witch left me alone with the roach. I was horrified and repulsed that I had to dance with this giant disgusting roach, but dance I did and suddenly the shell of the cockroach cracked open and out stepped a handsome young prince.

Her association to the cockroach was with her father, whom she looked down upon as disgusting and inferior and whose qualities she had rejected because they had turned sour in the soul. Her memories of him were primarily negative—that he came home in the middle of the night when the cockroaches were out; that he would often become violently irrational and unable to control his emotions. In reality he was also a very warm, outgoing, sensitive but mother-bound man who had not found his own strength and inner order to shape and form the intense feelings he had. He, himself, came from a home in which the father had not functioned and the mother was sick, so there was little in the way of modelling to help him. The daughter, seeing only the negative side of his sensitivity and outgoing feeling, had rejected all that in herself. When finally she had the courage to dance with the repulsive cockroach side and it cracked open, suddenly she had access to all the positive aspects of her father's feeling and sensitivity. But to get to this side of herself, she first had to face the negative, rejecting mother (the witch) and her rage at her father (the wild boar). The giant swan which took her there she associated with the swan which drew the raft of Lohengrin, preserver of the holy grail. So for her the way to spirit was to dance with the perverted figure, the cockroach.

One day while reading "The Yellow Dwarf,"[4] a fairy tale written by a woman, Madame d'Aulnoy, it struck me that this tale could very well be the story of a puella and her pitfalls if she does not develop her strengths and consciously face the perverted old man figure. It also suggests some steps of transformation. As the fairy tale begins, there is a queen who has only one daughter. Since the king is dead and the little princess is all that the mother cares for, the queen is afraid to lose her daughter's affections and so she pampers and spoils her, never trying to correct any of her faults. As a consequence the princess grows up very proud and vain, so much in love with her own beauty that she despises everyone else in the world. At first the queen is proud of all the attention from suitors that her daughter receives, but finally she is worried when the princess tells her she does not want to get married because none of her suitors are good enough for her. The queen begins to feel she was wrong in allowing her daughter to have her way so much, so she goes to consult a witch who is called "The Fairy of the Desert." To reach the fairy one must pass some terrible lions, so the queen takes along some cakes to give to them. But on the way she gets tired and falls asleep under an orange tree and somebody steals the cakes. She wakes up to the roar of the lions, and suddenly there is a yellow dwarf in the tree above her eating oranges. He says he will save her from the lions only if she promises her daughter in marriage to him. Because the queen is afraid, she agrees even though she is repulsed by him. At home again, the queen becomes very depressed and unhappy about her promise but tells no one what has happened. Finally the princess becomes worried about her mother and decides she will consult the fairy of the desert. She too falls asleep under the orange tree and, upon awakening, there finds the yellow dwarf. When he tells her what the queen has promised, she is repulsed. Then the lions appear, as they had to her mother, and to save herself, the princess agrees to marry the dwarf. The princess, whose name is Bellissima, returns home very sad.

Less proud after her encounter with the yellow dwarf, Bellissima decides to marry one of the suitors since it may be a way of getting rid of the yellow dwarf. She chooses to marry the King of the Gold Mines who, at first, in his insecurity, cannot believe it is he whom she has chosen. But he rejoices and soon she is really in love with him. The wedding day comes, but before the ceremony can take place, two intruders crash the party—the yellow dwarf and the fairy of the desert. The yellow dwarf challenges the King of the Gold Mines for the princess and the two fight. But the king loses courage and focus when he sees that the fairy of the desert, an ugly witch with snakes coiled around her head, has struck Bellissima senseless and is carrying her away. Giving up the fight with the yellow dwarf, the king rushes to save Bellissima or to die with her. In the end, however, he becomes so horrified at what is going on that he loses sight and consciousness and is carried away himself by the wicked fairy.

In the meantime the wicked fairy has changed her appearance to that of a beautiful woman, and Bellissima, who sees the king carried away by her, is grieved and jealous. The king, however, sees through the disguise and knows that he has to escape from the fairy and that to do so will take patience and cunning. Through flattery he gains the confidence of the witch so that she leaves him alone, and then a mermaid comes to him and helps him to escape. The mermaid tells him he will have many enemies to fight and gives him a special sword made from a diamond that will enable him to overcome all the enemies, provided he does not let the sword fall from his hand.

The king starts on his way to find Bellissima and first meets four terrible sphinxes that he has to kill and then six dragons with scales harder than iron, which he also must slay. This he does, but next he meets twenty-four pretty and graceful nymphs with garlands of flowers who bar his way. So he slays them, too, and finally he sees Bellissima. He rushes to her, but she draws away, feeling he has betrayed her. Hoping to show his love for her, he throws himself at her feet, but in doing so drops the sword. Whereupon the dwarf suddenly appears, grabs the sword, and stabs the king's heart. The princess, seeing her lover dead, dies of a broken heart.

In this fairy tale there is no father principle to begin with, and so the structure seems to me to reflect the situation a daughter might have with an absent or negligent father, insofar as there is no authority and no correction. The daughter is spoiled, having no sense of responsibility or commitment. She is Bellissima, the most beautiful of princesses, but she cannot love. The first real confrontation with a masculine principle in the story is with the yellow dwarf, a negative masculine figure. He blackmails both mother and daughter and wants to possess the daughter. Moreover, when he first appears, he is eating oranges from the tree where mother and daughter fall asleep, and if we were to take the tree as a symbol of life and growth and the oranges as a symbol of life's fruitfulness, it is the yellow dwarf who has possession of them and is eating them up. Neither the mother nor the daughter have developed within themselves consciousness, discipline, and courage, hence they fall asleep, lose the cakes, and are so afraid of the lion that they submit to the dwarf's victimization. What is lacking here is positive masculine development, i.e., the qualities of consciousness, discipline, courage, and decision-making. There has been no positive influence from the masculine principle. Rather it is undeveloped, leaving the way open for a take-over by the perverted influence from the dwarf, who victimizes the woman. The confrontation with the dwarf is not totally destructive, though, for it cuts into some of the princess' narcissism and pride. For the first time she makes a decision by committing herself to the king of the gold mines who is a potentially positive masculine principle. However, he is unsure of himself and so overly sensitive in the face of brutality that he loses consciousness and the ability to fight. Nevertheless, he is given another chance when the mermaid, a symbol of feminine wisdom, helps him escape and gives him her sword. The sword functions as a symbol of those qualities previously mentioned—it cuts through, hence makes distinctions and enables one to fight. In Tibetan Buddhism, the sword symbolizes the qualities of "Vajra confidence," a confidence which comes spontaneously from one's center; and in Christian symbolism it belongs to St. George, the hero who slays the dragon. It is also the sword that gives King Arthur the power to form the "round table," the place of communion and communication.

Using the sword, the king at first succeeds in combating his enemies: the sphinxes, dragons, and the pretty nymphs—

all symbolic of dangers coming from the unintegrated feminine realm. The negative sphinx mother puts impossible riddles that can't be solved and hence encourages indecisiveness; the dragon can devour with depression and inertia: and the pretty young nymphs seduce through naïvete and beauty. But in the end the king loses sight of his task when he tries to convince the princess that he loves her and attempts to patch up her wounded feelings. He is able to overcome his protection of the nymphs, but not of the princess. And so he gives in to her self-pity and feelings of betrayal and drops the sword, losing all the development and strength he had gained up to that point. Thus, there is no transformation in the end.

This fairy tale shows quite clearly, it seems to me, a picture of the way the undeveloped inner masculine side might look in a puella. On the one hand, there is the yellow dwarf, an image of the masculine in its perverted form, a figure who torments with self-doubt, self-pity, narcissism, depression, suicidal feelings, inertia, and so on. There is also the king of the gold mines, a figure with the potential to overcome this self-destruction, but who is undeveloped and too weak and sensitive to accomplish the task. What is lacking is the conscious focus and concentration on the task and the courageous strength, patience, and endurance to stick to it no matter what may happen.

As the fairy tale suggests, what the puella needs, regardless of her particular pattern, is to develop the warrior within, to learn to hold onto the sword. Karin Boye has expressed this in her poem, "A Sword."

A sword
flexible, supple and strong
a dancing sword
proudly obeying the stern laws
the hard rhythms in the steel.
A sword
I wanted to be—soul and body.

I hate this wretched willow soul of mine,
patiently enduring, plaited or twisted

by other hands.
I hate you
my lazy, dreamy soul.
You shall die.
Help me, my hate, sister of my longing
Help me be
a sword,
a dancing sword of tempered steel.[5]

In my work with the puella, I have found Castaneda's description of the "Warrior" to be invaluable.[6] Castaneda's books, in my view, describe many of the typically puerile attitudes to be found in individuals and in our culture. In the books these are expressed in the figure of Castaneda himself. His teacher, the Yaqui Indian Don Juan, constantly tries to show Castaneda his lack of commitment and courage and therefore inability to act in the world and be open to what is there. For example, Castaneda constantly plays the victim, indulges in self-pity about the past, romanticizes himself (thus taking himself too seriously), is impatient, fears taking responsibility for what he does, kills time without living it, complains, is bored, justifies himself, indulges in sentimentality, worries and clings to guilt, and so on. Like the puella of which he is the puer counterpart, he wastes his power in complaints, self-indulgence, and inertia. Don Juan tells Castaneda that he does all of these things to avoid taking responsibility for his decisions. But according to Don Juan there is no time for timidity, which clings to imagination and prevents one from acting now. Rather than complaint, indulgence, and self-pity, what is needed is to be a warrior! To make oneself strong takes no more work than to make oneself miserable, Don Juan says. Hence the warrior does not waste his time in weakness but takes responsibility for his acts and lives strategically, alert to synchronicity and to what is. The warrior is not afraid because he is guided by unbending purpose, is focused and alert—hence he can cope with all threats and terrors. To hold onto himself yet let go of himself at the same time—that is the way of the warrior.

Thus he embodies the integration of the receptive and creative, living and loving the paradoxes of life, balancing both the terror and the wonder of being human. Rather than falling into the frequent pattern of puella innocence and seduction which covers up a hidden hostility and aggression, the direct confrontation requires an assertion which is as focused and alert as Castaneda's image of the warrior—a readiness to stand on one's own ground and to be open to what is there. And in that opening, just as the cockroach was transformed, one may find that the perverted old man was only a cover-up for the youthful vigor and wisdom of the prince within, waiting for the woman to care for that new-found strength. Perhaps the puella needs to remember these words of the poet Rilke, who speaks of a similar pattern, though as it functions in the masculine psyche:

> How should we be able to forget those ancient myths that are at the beginning of all peoples, the myths about dragons that at the last moment turn into princesses; perhaps all the dragons of our lives are princesses who are only waiting to see us once beautiful and brave. Perhaps everything terrible is in its deepest being something helpless that wants help from us.[7]

2. THE AMAZON, THE ANGRY BOY, AND THE DUMMLING

For a woman who is in the grips of an armored-Amazon reaction, the armor can sometimes get awfully heavy. To carry around the heavy weight of achievement, duty, martyrdom, or militancy can be awfully burdensome indeed. Seen by the collective eye, the Amazon has a venerable position. She has worked and suffered, frequently denying her impulses in lieu of a more worthy goal. She has been both responsible and righteous. Like Atlas, she has figuratively carried the world on her shoulders. No wonder, then, that her shoulders and back begin to get tired, sometimes collapse, and the armor begins to crack. But behind the armor, behind

105

the strong and impressive persona, one often discovers deep in the psyche a sensitive, rebellious, and angry boy—angry because he is weak, neglected, and put down as a "dummling." This image of the angry boy I have found to be a frequent figure in the psyche of the armored Amazon; i.e., the woman who has opted for a strong masculine ego-adaptation.

I found this figure in myself one day in a dream, shortly before I began analysis. At that time I had just finished the arduous task of obtaining a Ph.D. in philosophy. I was also married, but my husband and I lived as two "bachelors" focused on work. I had also accepted a view that women were no different from men, and while numerous urges and feelings contradicted this idea, I felt guilty and so suppressed them. Needless to say, I was quite depressed. In the dream, a redhaired twelve-year-old boy was sitting behind me on a grassy hill, throwing small, hard, sharp stones which were hitting my back and shoulders. He was obviously angry at me, trying to get my attention, and he finally succeeded. Shortly after that I went into analysis; my defended professional world cracked apart; and I was confronted with that angry boy's feelings.

Here, I am not talking about the positive side of the Amazon, for her confidence, assertiveness, and accomplishment in the world are extremely valuable indeed. Rather, I am speaking of those women who have assumed an Amazonic posture out of a reaction against inadequate fathering, i.e., of women who feel the burden of this role, who are exhausted from the battle and the work, and who have lost the sense of meaning they had once found in it. In these cases, the loss of meaning and exhaustion suggest that things have become too rigid and serious. Where is the fun, the play, the spontaneity? The playful boyish side seems to be lost, but it is my experience that he is hiding in the figure of the angry and rebellious boy. That the boyish side has been lost is not very surprising if a woman's experience of this side of the masculine has been fraught with disappointment, unreliability, worry, or shame. The experience of throwing out the baby with the bathwater is as common as the saying, so to throw out the positive, inspiring side of the youthful man as a reaction to the dangerous and disgusting side happens frequently. As in the case of the puella, I think this happens when the father principle has been experienced as undeveloped and/or distorted. But rather than remaining passive and looking for the father in another, the Amazonic woman tries to incorporate it in herself. As she tries to become her own father, her ego-adaptation correspondingly tends to become masculine. While ultimately the integration of the father principle is essential in a woman's development, what happens in the case of the Amazon's reaction is an identification with that part of the masculine which is sober and serious, strong and powerful, efficient and accomplished, dutiful and responsible. The playful, spontaneous, imaginative, and entertaining youthful side is usually neglected and devalued. No wonder that he gets angry and mean.

One way the angry boy can disrupt the Amazon's life is to get her in trouble with the collective. Often when one compulsively tries to do everything right—driving a car; for example—along comes a trickster who leads you the wrong way on a one-way street and there are the police behind, ready to give a traffic ticket. Another way is via the body, as when the body rebels against overwork in the form of symptoms, such as ulcers, colitis, headaches, or an aching, strained back and neck. A depression that makes it difficult to work may also have an angry boy behind it, as might a situation in which one makes a blunder and ends up looking ridiculous. Sometimes the angry boy's attack happens blatantly on the outer level.

After several hours of trying to write about this very subject, I was driving very slowly down the street when two adolescent boys who were playing on the opposite side of the street directed a mechanical toy car under my car so suddenly that it was quite impossible to stop. My car ran over their toy, and they got very angry. Instead of really confronting them with my own anger at their irresponsibility and perhaps consequently gaining some understanding of them,

I drove on to the beach where I was headed and parked my car. When I came back, I discovered raw egg smeared all over my windshield and car, no doubt the work of these two angry boys. I felt angry, helpless, and humiliated. Often, as a result of the angry boy's attack, there results this feeling of ridiculousness and vulnerability. Quite literally, these angry young boys had "egged me on." Upon reflection, I realized that not only had I run over a toy, symbolic of my suppressed youthful side, I was also afraid of the collective authorities, the police. For immediately in my imagination I had wondered if one could get a traffic ticket for running over a toy car. I had been made to be a fool by these angry young boys and yet I had also learned quite a bit about myself.

In my experience, the transformation of the rebellious boy figure lies in the image of the "fool" or the "dummling." One finds this figure in many fairy tales in which there is a youngest son who appears stupid, bumbling, and incapable in comparison to his older brothers who are handsome, strong, and capable and who deride their younger dummling brother with sarcastic cynicism. Yet, in the fairy tale it is the dummling who is able to complete the task and not the stronger brothers.

I will look at a dummling tale shortly, but first here is a concrete example of how the dummling helped me. In the process of writing on the Amazon, my own Amazonic side got stirred up and with it an inner rebellious boy who enticed me into a series of accidents and other unpleasant and embarrassing events. During this period, too, my dream life revealed a pathological teenager who kept trying to break into my apartment. Instead of asking him what he wanted, I shot some mace at him, but the mace got into my eyes too. Although I was by now aware that the angry boy was out to get my Amazon, I nevertheless signed up for a strenuous twenty-mile hike; and I got up at the arduous hour of 6 a.m. in order to be sure of arriving in plenty of time. As I was driving to the starting place, this conflict of Amazon-angry boy was on my mind. With all my preparation, I did get to the starting place in plenty of time, and the hike leader gave me instructions on where to park my car and how to get back to the hike's starting place. But, despite the directions, I got lost, and by the time I retraced my path, the hikers had gone. I was irate! Hadn't I done the heroic thing, getting up so early, etc? But then I decided to go on my own walk and suddenly it struck me that this twenty-mile hike was a rather Amazonic project for me at that time. My rebellious boy-side had interfered again, this time in the aspect of the dummling linked conveniently to my inferior ability to follow detailed directions. Finally I accepted the situation and sat down in the sun by a stream and started to write—a more creative kind of writing than I had ever done before. So although the rebellious dummling figure obstructed my ego plans of the day, actually he helped me to a creative way which I hadn't yet reached on my own.

The Amazonic reaction to the negative father, it seems to me, denies the dummling because the "weak" aspect of the male is so unacceptable to her. And so she stresses the strong, heroic element in herself. But then she loses all the positive side—the spontaneity and gentle unpredictability, the bumbling mistakes that seem stupid to the efficient collective eye, but which often take one into just the unexpected spot that gives meaning. Although the dummling figure usually is ridiculed in everyday life by the collective (which the Amazon often serves), in film he is loved. We have only to think of examples such as Charlie Chaplin or Buster Keaton or Peter Sellers. Not only are they endearing figures, they are also "heroes," though not from the collective viewpoint. Like the Fool in the Tarot, they are important to the individuation process because they have given up ego success orientation and that enables the new creative element to enter. When all the known ways fail, the dummling bumbles into a new solution because he is not fixed in his ways. He is open!

If one looks at fairy tales in which the dummling figure appears, some essential features emerge. Quite often, for example, the dummling knows he can't perform an impossible task and so, instead of trying to "prove himself," he just sits down and weeps. He is able to acknowledge his weakness and vulnerability and is not ashamed of it. Usually he trusts that help will come and he is able to wait. He also has a good heart and shares whatever he has. The animals are his friends and help him because he in turn is kind to them, helping and giving to them when he can. The dummling is also invariably the youngest brother who is put down by the older brothers. He tends not to speak in defense since he knows how to wait in silence. Perhaps his most central quality is his receptivity. He doesn't need to control. The dummling follows the feather, which when tossed into the air yields to the natural air currents; he is open and receptive to nature and its flow—he is able to wait and not force things. And so he can be open to unknown and new things that appear in his field of vision. That he is not afraid of appearing foolish before the collective eye enables him to act with trust and be receptive to what comes.

In the Grimm's fairy tale "The Golden Goose," we find just such a dummling.[8] Called "Dummling" or "Simpleton" by his family, he is the youngest of three sons and is "despised, mocked, and sneered at on every occasion." The older brothers are very clever and sensible and follow their own ego plans. Each takes a trip to the forest to fetch some wood, and their mother gives them sweet cakes and wine so they won't be hungry or thirsty. Each of the two older sons are very careful to protect their own food and drink, and so when they meet a little grey-haired man who asks for some, they refuse. But then the one brother cuts his arm with an axe, and the other cuts his leg, and each has to be taken home. Dummling then asks his father if he can cut wood, and the father says he is too stupid. But finally the father consents, saying that maybe Dummling will get wiser if he hurts himself. Instead of sweet cake and wine, his mother gives him a cinder cake and some sour beer, and Dummling goes to the forest where he meets the little old man who asks him for some food and drink. Dummling tells him what it is, but is willing to share what he has. When they begin to eat, the food has become sweet cake and wine. Because Dummling has a good heart and shares what he has, the old man promises he will bring him good luck. So when Dummling cuts down a tree, he finds in its roots a goose with golden feathers. Taking the goose with him, he attracts a group of people, each of whom wants to take a golden feather. But when each one tries to get the feather, the hand sticks to the goose. Dummling just ignores these people and continues with his goose, and soon he has a trail of people running behind him, all stuck to the goose. He then comes to a city ruled by a king whose daughter is so serious no one can make her laugh. The worried king decrees that whoever can make his daughter laugh shall marry her and inherit the kingdom. Upon hearing this, Dummling takes his goose and the following train of people to the king's daughter. As soon as she sees them, the princess laughs and laughs and laughs, unable to stop. Then Dummling asks the king for his daughter's hand, but the king doesn't want Dummling for a son-in-law, and so he sets several impossible tasks: to produce a man who can drink a cellarful of wine; to produce another who can eat a mountain of bread; and, finally, to produce a ship which can sail on land or water. For each task, Dummling heads straight for the forest where he finds the little man whom he has helped and in turn this little man helps him perform the tasks. After all three tasks have been completed, the king realizes Dummling is more powerful than he thought and that he can't prevent him from marrying his daughter. So Dummling marries the daughter whom he has helped to laugh and eventually becomes king.

This fairy tale shows an image of a daughter stuck in an Amazon armor—she is so serious she cannot laugh. Her father devalues Dummling to the extent that even after he makes the daughter laugh, Dummling is still not good enough. The tale also shows that only the masculine figures who are practical and follow their own ego plans are honored by the parents—only the clever elder brothers are trusted and given good cake and wine. But the tale also shows that though the elder brothers may be sensible and goal directed, it is their over-emphasis on achievement that causes them

111

injury and prevents them from bringing back the wood. In the same way, a well-armored Amazonic woman who is controlling is likely to find that she doesn't know how to go into the forest (symbolic of the unconscious or inner unknown) and bring back the fuel which could ignite her creativity and passion. It takes the dishonored, naïve, and supposedly stupid, dummling figure to be able to go into the forest and bring back a treasure. He does this through his nonpossessive generosity, which is not directed towards any goal or object. Yet, the paradox is that through his nonpossessiveness he gains access to the help of the little old man in the forest and to the treasure hidden in the tree. What he finds in the roots of the tree is the goose with golden feathers which fascinates all who see it. The goose, of course, is a silly creature, according to common opinion, but this image shows there is gold in the foolishness. The gold, however, cannot be grasped by ego-control or by possessiveness, and so all who try to do this become stuck to the goose's golden feathers. What a striking image to show how one can get "stuck" by trying to grasp and hold onto things! It is the calculating attitude that turns out to be ridiculous and not the dummling's naïve way. In fact, it is now the dummling who is in charge, and he proceeds on his way despite all the people stuck to the goose. Here one sees that although he may seem stupid, there is really a trickster aspect to the dummling. He knows all these people are stuck, but he just continues on. So, he is not without a shadow element for he doesn't really try to help all of those stuck people. But sometimes it is just the shadow aspect which is needed to crack open a rigid situation. Right here, when the dummling continues on leading the trail of stuck people, I see the angry boy aspect in the dummling. Here they work together to transform a serious, stiff, and stuck form of femininity into a youthful, laughing one. A woman stuck in an Amazon armor is usually too serious to laugh. But if she can let loose and see the value of the goose-like foolishness and begin to laugh at the attitudes that try to possess and control and thereby keep her stuck in her armor, then the Amazon armor can crack open and marriage with the dummling is possible.

The force of a negative father influence leading to an Amazon armor reaction formation is shown in the tale by the fact that even after the dummling is able to make her laugh, the father still refuses him and sets even more seemingly impossible tasks. The nature of each task is significant since each involves indulgence and/or going beyond limits, e.g., drinking a cellarful of wine, eating a mountain of bread, etc. Going beyond limits is just what the over-emphasized control orientation would never allow a woman identified with that aspect to do. So in a way the father principle, personified by the king, ultimately helps. Although on one level the king devalues the dummling, on another level he requires the very tasks that caricature the old heroic identification—tasks which will loosen up the limiting side and allow the entertaining, more indulgent youthful side to be. The dummling is able to do these tasks because he has the help of the old man in the forest, a wise old masculine figure in the unconscious. So here we have a psychological integration of the old man and young boy who can act together in the world consciously and capably, in contrast to the angry and rebellious eruption of a repressed boyish side from the unconscious, reacting against a too rigid ego structure. With this cooperation between the old man and the youngest son, the old ruling structure can be replaced by a new one—the dummling can be the new king.

The intertwining of Amazon, angry boy, and dummling is illustrated in the following case of a young Swiss woman who worked with me in analysis a number of years ago. She came from a family in which the father was weak and debilitated by a respiratory illness but who nevertheless ruled the family with an attitude of patriarchal authority which devalued the feminine. "Kirche, Kinder, Kuche" (Church, Children, Kitchen); woman's place was only in the home. As a result of this view of women, and the way she was treated because of it, this young woman felt worthless, trapped, and unfree in the "feminine role." Her mother also went along with the father by being a dutiful wife and submitting to this patriarchal view of femininity, a view which the Swiss culture enforced. At that time, women in Switzerland could not even vote! As an adolescent she was forced into the dutiful role when her father demanded she leave school and undertake instead an apprenticeship to train to be a housekeeper. Cut off from her chances to study, she became a hard worker and inevitably fell into relationships with male university students whom she then undertook to support financially. At the same time she resented this and the feminine role that had been thrust upon her. Feeling it to be worthless, she denied her feminine side. In her attitudes, she alternated between the Amazonic modes of martyr and militant, and the puella modes of misfit and high flyer. Nevertheless, she continued to support her boyfriends and did not develop herself. She would support a man for a while and then suddenly he would run off with another girl, always a university student. After several of these experiences, she came into analysis.

Under the veneer of her competent, efficient, cheery, and responsible persona was a very vulnerable girl with a lot of anger and resentment. Her "angry boy" had emerged quite early during puberty when she stole fruits from the family garden, for which her authoritarian father punished her severely. Later her anger came out against the Swiss government and the police. During this period she took part in several demonstrations and, in one, suffered from severe tear gassing. The resulting helplessness and humiliation were the most injurious to her. For the most part, however, her anger was directed against herself in the form of a very low self-image which prevented her from developing her potentialities. Instead, she continued to work in martyr fashion supporting her boyfriends while they developed themselves. Secretly she resented this and looked down upon them, but kept on working and denying her needs. In the course of analysis, she was able to bring out this anger and to start developing a talent in one of the arts.

This young woman's Amazon armor covered up a shame of her femininity so that she overrode the demands and needs of her body. She also mouthed a theory that there was really no difference between men and women. And she treated her body that way, not acknowledging the changes of body and mood brought on by her menstrual periods. In stoic determination she forced herself to work even harder during those times, but ironically the work she did was in service to her boyfriends, and not for her own self-development.

The motif of the dummling fooling the armored Amazon came up in the following dream. In it she was crossing a central bridge in Zurich when suddenly to her surprise she found a tampax in her mouth. Embarrassed, she quickly threw it over her shoulder into the river on her right. But then she heard peals of laughter from a crowd of people lined up along the banks of the river, most of whom were women university students. They were all laughing and pointing to her and then to something in the river. When she looked she saw the tampax which had now expanded to a giant size. Unable to bear the humiliation, she tried to run away, but awoke while the people were still laughing at her.

The dream brought things to a focus, showing that her theories about women did not really correspond to her bodily and emotional needs. The fact that the tampax was out of place, i.e., in her mouth rather than her vagina, suggested that the needs of her feminine nature were not in their proper place. That she threw the tampax away behind her suggested that she suppressed her feminine needs and didn't want to look at them. But even the women whom in reality she admired and wanted to be like (the women university students) were laughing at her denial. And the giant size of the tampax suggested that her denial only made the problem larger. Whereas her idea of woman's nature was to be just like a man and to be totally independent emotionally, in reality she was very dependent on every man with whom she lived, serving their needs rather than her own. Although she criticized her parents' ideas of the feminine role, and rightly so, she was living out that very pattern by supporting her boyfriends instead of developing herself. She was angry at the Swiss collective for their view of women, and her anger was justified. But because it was congealed in the form of rebellion, it was not effective. It took being a dummling in the dream to enable her to see all of this. Shortly after this dream, she had a series of dreams of being pregnant and having a baby, which brought out her desire at a very deep level to have a child. But her ideas about women would not allow it. Ultimately she broke out of her martyr-misfit pattern in relationships, married a man who was more sensitive to her needs, eventually had a baby, and continued to work on her artistic potentialities.

What the dummling brings to the woman trapped in an Amazon armor is a receptive, letting-be attitude which enables her to enjoy the simple things and just move in the life flow. To quote a Haiku poem by Issa:

> Spring unfolds anew...
> Now in my second childhood
> Folly, Folly, too[9]

3. THE MAN WITH HEART

When the perverted old man and the angry boy are identified and faced, and when the warrior and dummling sides are allowed to be, quite frequently a new masculine image spontaneously emerges in dreams and imagination. Quite often such a figure first appears in dreams as an intruder, a stranger who breaks into the woman's home. While I was in the midst of working with these figures via my writing, I had three successive dreams of a young male intruder. Each was also connected to nature. One man brought a cat and dog with him. Another took me bathing in a clear mountain lake. And the third decorated a new room in my home with colorful handwoven rugs from his travels, vibrant with flower and bird designs. These dream men brought me heart and glowing feeling. They liked the feminine side of me and expressed it with their gifts. Now I had a masculine figure in myself who liked me as a woman. No longer did I have to be the innocent sweet daughter or the super-competent wonder woman. No longer was the masculine reduced to son and father. Now there was also a loving man.

116

I would like to share with you my fantasy of "The Man with Heart," for he is the positive *inner* masculine figure that a healthy relation with the father provides. First, he is caring, warm, and strong. He is not afraid of anger, nor is he afraid of intimacy and love. He can see beyond the bewitchment, beyond the artificial defensive appearances to the essential me within. He stays by me and is patient. But he initiates, confronts, and moves on as well. He is stable and enduring. Yet his stability comes from flowing with the stream of life, from being in the moment. He plays and works and enjoys both modes of being. He feels at home wherever he is—in the inner spaces or the outer world. He is a man of the earth—instinctual and sexy. He is a man of the spirit—soaring and creative. He loves nature: animals, birds, flowers, the woods and mountain meadows, the rivers and the sea. He loves children and the inner child. And he appreciates the cyclic seasons of time. He can revel in the blossoming of spring's early flowering, relax and linger in summer's stronger ripening, mature in autumn's colorful last blaze, and deepen in winter's snowy silence, opening up once more to spring's rebirth. He loves beauty—art, the word, and music. Perhaps he even sings or plays the bassoon or violin. And he dances to life's rhythms. He is the soul-mate, the inner friend and lover who accompanies a woman on the journey and adventure of life.

II.

THE HURTING

You stand at the blackboard, daddy,
In the picture I have of you.
A cleft in your chin instead of your foot
But no less a devil for that, no not
Any less the black man who

Bit my pretty red heart in two.
I was ten when they buried you.
At twenty I tried to die
And get back, back, back to you.
I thought even the bones would do.

But they pulled me out of the sack,
And they stuck me together with glue.
And then I knew what I had to do.
I made a model of you,
A man in black with a Meinkampf look

And a love of the rack and the screw.
And I said I do, I do.
So daddy, I'm finally through.
The black telephone's off at the root,
The voices just can't worm through.

If I've killed one man, I've killed two.
The vampire who said he was you
And drank my blood for a year,
Seven years, if you want to know.
Daddy, you can lie back now.

There's a stake in your fat black heart
And the villagers never liked you.
They are dancing and stomping on you.
They always knew it was you.
Daddy, daddy, you bastard, I'm through.

Sylvia Plath
"Daddy"

CHAPTER SIX

RAGE

Say to the upright men
in the world
that they must harvest
your ripened hate
and plough the field of your fury
before they will see your face.
Cecil Bødker

Rage can release the wounded woman, for her wound has a burning center that stings and hurts. Some women repress the hurt and the anger that goes with it. And then that anger turns inward, perhaps in the form of bodily symptoms or depressive suicidal thoughts that paralyze their lives and their creativity. Others let their rage out, but run over people in the process. In their hurt, they hurt others. No matter in which direction the rage goes, it is unfocused, unformed, and explosive. But it also carries powerful energy which, if utilized well, could release their potentiality as women. Rage can be a central force for redeeming the father and transforming the feminine.

The following dream shows dramatically the full force of rage which many women must confront in themselves, and it also shows the structure of the masculine within when it is destructively split into unrelated opposites.

A man friend and I were going riding. We found our horses near a strange stable. My red mare was saddled and bridled, but loose and unattended. As I came up to her, she started to run away. But she stepped on her reins and her head jerked against the bit. Suddenly she panicked and went into a rage and reared up on her hind legs. Now she was as big as a giant and was half human and I saw that she was crazy. She grabbed a girl nearby and squeezed her out of her skin like one can squeeze sausage meat out of its skin. The girl was dead. Then the mare rushed toward me in a wild rage. I looked to my friend for help, but he was so horrified and helpless that he could only vomit. I called to the stable man, but he paid no attention to me. I woke up in horror as this raging red mare came towards me.

The force and strength of the rage is unmistakable in this powerful image of the giant, half-human, psychotic red mare. The dream also shows clearly two inadequate modes of masculine reaction: the brutally indifferent figure of the stable man, and the sensitive but incapacitated friend. There is no saving masculine figure in the dream. The only other figure, aside from the dreamer herself, is a helpless young girl without substance. She has no real center and so can be squeezed out of her skin as a woman with no genuine inner strength might fall apart if confronted directly. The dreamer is left to confront the crazy red horse head on. For the dreamer, the crazy red horse was an image of her father's unbridled passion and rage when he was out of control. The red horse symbolized her own passion and rage as well. The stable man she saw as the brutally indifferent side of her father and the incapacitated friend as his weak, sensitive side. Both were also sides of herself which were ineffective in dealing with the raging energy she felt within. At the time of the dream, the brutally indifferent stable man, in the form of a perfectionist inner judge, had been in control and had just dropped the reins. The old ego-adaptation was at its end. The friend, who was a sensitive and feeling man, was still an undeveloped figure in herself, not strong enough to help. So the energy was powerfully present, but not yet directed—

hence its loose-reined, dangerously frenzied state. Because she had seen her father in crazy rages so often, out of control and unable to function in the world, she was terribly afraid of that side of herself. She was afraid of a breakdown, afraid she might go crazy one day, and suffered from terrible anxiety attacks. As a child, she had little protection against this father out of control, and so she resorted to a rigid defense system that protected her from the strength of her feeling and passion. And that had resulted in a helpless, pleasing girl without substance and a thin-skinned persona that couldn't hold against stress and so she could be squeezed out of her skin. When the brutal, indifferent stable man dropped the reins that were controlling her horse, the girl without substance was doomed to destruction. Something new had to happen with all that raging energy. The dreamer had to confront it consciously and directly! This woman needed to allow her passionate, fiery feeling side to be, to assume responsibility for it, and to learn to direct it.

The raging red horse symbolized wild, undirected energy and the dreamer was terrified of it. This fear of rage is common to many women. If her father has been eaten up by rage himself, then the daughter is left with the unsolved rage of the father. She may have experienced the father losing all control in fits of rage and have been directly terrified by him. Or, the father's rage may have been suppressed, either in a passive, nonassertive way, or in a rigidly controlled way. In either case the right relation to rage was not there as a model. Neither suppression of rage nor uncontrolled explosions can effectively carry the full force of the energy. The father, lost to rage, betrays the father archetype insofar as the order, stability, and confident relation to the world usually provided by the father is disrupted. And a woman's relation to sexuality and the creative forces of the unconscious are often threatened as well. The "other," the "unknown," often becomes fearsome rather than fascinating. And all the creative energy released by sexuality and the mysterious unknown is suspect and often paralyzed. Moreover, if a woman has experienced anger as pathological in her father, she often suspects her own anger is pathological too. And to avoid confrontation with this powerful and possibly pathological force, she often veils her rage.

Rage can be veiled in many ways. One way is via addictions. With alcohol, the rage can come out when one is drunk, but without the conscious and responsible acceptance of it. Overeating may be another way of "throwing one's weight around." Rage is often hidden in the body. Many women suffer from hypochondria, experiencing physical weakness and illness that really cover pent-up energy. Headaches, backaches, ulcers, colitis, and stomach problems frequently disappear when anger is accepted. Depression, a state in which all one's energy seems to disappear, is still another subterfuge for rage. Anxiety attacks often cover up anger that leaves one shaking in helplessness. Suicidal tendencies veil a murderous anger turned toward oneself, and in the form of emotional blackmail, veil anger towards the other. Many women veil their rage through sexual seduction and/or rejection. And some provoke rage in others, letting the other person act it out for them. The bitter, cynical attitude many women have of "taking the man for all he's worth" is a way of angrily getting back at him for keeping them dependent. This often entails compulsive shopping and spending which consumes energy and time. Obsessive guilt feelings also veil rage for they are like beating oneself incessantly. Another frequent way of covering up anger is through the intellect via a "know-it-all" attitude that intimidates others, or a critical attack that is not really to the point emotionally and leaves the other person helpless. Martyrdom, asceticism, a puritanical work ethic, pride about one's sense of duty and responsibility all can be ways of hiding one's anger. And so can the brazen, self-righteous attitude that says to the other, "I am who I am," all the while afraid to risk showing vulnerability.

Puella women tend to be afraid of the fiery rage of self-assertion. So often they go to extremes to placate the other and adapt, hiding their rage under a pleasing persona, and the rage comes out in some of the above forms. But then they feel alienated from themselves and cheated in the end. In giving over their energy to others, they become depleted and lose their center, feeling weak and helpless. Rage can also be suppressed under an Amazon armor that appears seemingly strong on the outer level, creating a wall between oneself and others. But the positive power of the rage is lost because the armor is in the way. In both cases, the rage needs to be recognized and released before it can be transformed.

Often when there is a great deal of rage resulting from a negative relation to the father, that rage is experienced also with one's lover. And frequently it is hard to handle ordinary anger, as in the following example. Last Valentine's Day, three women I worked with had a similar experience: all were neglected in one way or another by their lovers. All three were hurt and enraged. One got drunk and angrily told her lover off. Another held her anger in and fell into a deep depression and hopelessness. And the third fell into a hysterical fit. None of these ways of expressing anger were very effective. None of the women felt they really reached their lover. Each woman was unable to direct her anger in a conscious and effective way because there was unresolved rage in the past and no adequate model to show them how to deal with it. And due to that unintegrated rage that came from their childhood, they couldn't handle their present anger with their lovers. When the rage isn't consciously integrated, it often results in an unconscious attack on the partner, criticizing the other unmercifully and destroying all possibility for love.

Behind the rage are often tears, as was the case with these three women. Underneath the anger is vulnerability and the possibility for tenderness and intimacy. And sometimes, because of the rejection and abandonment experienced from the father's rage, the tears and tenderness are veiled along with the rage. So if a woman can learn to relate to her rage, this may open up her tender side and the possibility for an intimate relationship. Frequently when women express

125

their anger with their lovers, they open up more sexually as well. So rage can allow a fuller love experience on both the physical and emotional levels.

Sometimes the rage comes from the mother. In these cases the father is usually afraid of his own rage and doesn't confront the rage in the mother. Rene's father sacrificed her in this way by being too nice and pleasing. He didn't stand up to her mother's anger and self-destructive tendencies. He loved his daughter, but this only made the mother more jealous. Like her father, the daughter tried to please and this became her pattern. But no matter how hard she tried, she was never able to please her mother. Rene was especially afraid of her mother's anger. When Rene was in her teens, her mother began drinking heavily, became more hostile, made several suicide attempts, and finally had a nervous breakdown. During this time the father was not an active force in the home and set no limits on the mother's behavior. He was unable to say: "NO!" I will not take this behavior from you."

Rene coped with this situation by seeking substitute mother figures outside the family and by being very adaptable, pleasing, and responsible. But underneath she was secretly afraid she was like her mother. Her pleasing persona and charm worked well during her twenties and early thirties, when she was married to an older man who was an "eternal boy." The relationship was pleasant and they never fought, but it lacked depth; finally both partners lost interest. Then she became involved with a different kind of man, one who was very practical and who criticized her when she over-extended herself and didn't keep appointments on time or do things right. In this relationship there were many fights. Although she loved this man deeply, she couldn't cope with his anger or her own, and this brought her into analysis. Her pattern of pleasing didn't work in this relationship, and she realized she would have to learn to fight back. But fighting secretly frightened her, for she was so afraid of becoming like her mother.

Her father had given her no preparation and guidance for aggression. For a model, she had only her mother's hysterical rage which had tyrannized the whole family. During this period she had a dream that she and her father were taken captive by some ferocious medieval soldiers and were thrown in a pit where together they watched a horrible, bloody battle going on above them. This dream was symbolic of the uncontrollable primitive rage of her mother and the helplessness which she and her father experienced in the face of this rage.

When confronted with anger, she would fall into a deep depression. And since her self-confidence was low, she would often blame herself for the fight. She began to compensate by becoming more and more responsible and perfectionistic, both in the relationship and her job. She tended to set impossible goals, and promised to do so many things that she couldn't meet all of her obligations. The result was that she became very anxious and frantic, afraid she would collapse under the pressure. Behind all this was the fear that she was like her mother and would end up in a nervous collapse, unable to function. I felt that the anxiety, resulting from her tendency to please and over-extend herself to avoid anger, veiled the hidden rage with which she had never learned to deal. Having seen only the hysterics of her mother and the helplessness of her father, she had learned no models of control. She also suffered from a lack of confidence, doubting her self-worth, and so she was afraid to assert herself. This woman needed to see the value in the rage she feared. Rene also needed to set limits for herself and others and to say: "NO! I cannot do that." But in order to set limits she had to value herself.

Dreams gave her an image. In one dream an elegantly dressed Russian queen sat regally in a carriage drawn by four magnificent, prancing horses. This queen was a woman who knew what she wanted and was not afraid to assert herself and demand her rights. The queen knew how to control and guide the energy of the horses to go where she

127

wanted. Previously in the dream Rene had to confront a huge gorilla that had been following her around, and it took this confrontation before she was able to see the queen. Symbolically this meant that confronting the powerful gorilla force of her aggression was required in order to get in contact with the regal, queenly power she had within herself.

This woman was also cut off from her own power to rage—her "Kali power." Kali is the Hindu goddess of creation and destruction. Her rage can destroy, but it also can create. And so it can provide the fire for transformation. Kali's power to rage symbolizes the power many women need to develop in themselves—the power to assert themselves, to set their own limits, and to say no when necessary.[1]

Rage can also release spirit. Sometimes it is even necessary to rage against "God," against the tragic forces of destiny, in order to raise consciousness to a higher level. In Jung's view, when Job, after years of patient suffering, finally gave vent to his fury against the injustice of God, the consciousness not only of all mankind but even of the divine was raised.[2] In my own experience, at this level the rage acknowledges both one's vulnerability and weakness as well as one's power and strength, paradoxically uniting these opposites and thus achieving a transformation of the previous level of being and consciousness. My own outraged outbursts against the destructive legacy I had inherited from my father invariably infused me with the energy to act and try to change that negative karmic pattern, insofar as that was possible. And it also brought me closer to my father for I felt with more compassion the life and death struggle to which he finally succumbed.

How can the wounded woman connect with such powerful rage instead of being threatened and terrified of it? And how can she transform the rage into creative energy? In my experience, there are at least two stages: first getting the rage out and then transforming the power of the anger into creative energy. The fairy tale "The Frog Prince" shows what can happen when rage breaks into the open. And the myth "Psyche and Amor" suggests a way towards transformation.

128

Quite often the wounded woman is afraid of the fire and energy raging within. But the analogy to the way one deals with a forest fire may be apt. There one "fights fire with fire." The forest fighters actually set a fire around the dangerous fire in order to limit it. In the same way, letting the rage out into the open with a burst of feeling can actually limit rage by releasing it. For rage can be an act of assertion that sets limits and establishes identity by saying, "I won't take any more of this!" Confronting the suppressed rage with rage is suggested by the Grimm Brothers' version of the fairy tale "The Frog Prince."[3]

In that tale, a princess, whose golden ball has rolled away down into a well, has asked a frog to help retrieve her ball. The frog agrees to do so if the princess in return will feed and care for him and allow him in her bed. Once the princess has her ball back, she forgets about her promise. But while she is eating dinner with her father, there is a loud croak outside the door. Her father inquires who is there, and after he hears the frog's story, he tells his daughter she must keep her promise. The princess is repulsed by the frog, but takes him to her room and feeds him. To take him to bed with her is too repugnant, and so she leaves him on the floor. When the frog demands his due, the total fulfillment of the promise, she becomes enraged and throws him angrily against the wall, whereupon he is transformed into a prince, his original form before bewitchment.

Here rage is the appropriate response. It releases the prince from his perverted frog form. This way may be especially appropriate for the puella who needs to confront rage. For in becoming enraged herself, she experiences the full force of her own strength and power, which previously she gave over to others. She also defies patriarchal authority. Throwing the frog back against the wall is like throwing back projections that don't really fit; for example, throwing back a negative projection that women are passive and powerless. One frequent pitfall of the puella is that she accepts projections of powerlessness. But then the power she really has, the power of her feminine feeling and instinct, degenerates and often turns against herself. She is likely to be angry about her loss of power but, at the same time, afraid to show it. And so to avoid confrontation with self and others, she may veil her rage. But when the rage is veiled, its effective power is lost.

In "The Frog Prince" fairy tale, the princess takes responsibility for her rage when she throws the frog against the wall. She pays attention to her feminine instincts and feelings and trusts them when she acts on her feeling of repulsion and disobeys her father's orders. When she first met the frog, she was a helpless little girl who let her golden ball roll away from her, as so many women lose access to the strong center of their feminine spirit. And as a helpless girl, she made a promise she didn't want to keep. How true this is of many women who exchange their independence for the promise of security and material well-being. This happened too in the fairy tale "The Yellow Dwarf," where the princess feels helpless before the rage of the oncoming lions and promises to marry the perverted dwarf in order to save her life. But in that fairy tale the princess never directly confronts the lions or the dwarf and is doomed to self-destruction through her feelings of helplessness and self-pity. In "The Frog Prince" there is transformation because the princess finally takes responsibility for her feminine feelings and asserts them. In an act of rage, she redeems the frog and transforms him into a prince. When she asserts herself and throws the frog against the wall, he turns into her lover. So the possibility of intimate relationship happens along with the rage.

Women today need to do this not only in their personal lives but on the cultural level as well. Many women in our time are angry because their feminine values have been put down. They need to assert themselves forcefully out of their own feminine experience, and this may take a few angry outbursts. Some of the cultural frogs (the projections and prejudices) need to be thrown against the wall. But ultimately this expression of rage needs to be not only forceful but formed and focused effectively as well. And this conscious awareness of one's energy and how one wants to use it may keep women from making those original false promises that keep them helpless. In learning to relate to their rage, they may raise the level of consciousness about the unresolved cultural rage which at its worst leads to war and persecution.

"The Frog Prince" is a story of rage breaking out, a rage which can be the beginning of consciousness. But when women begin to become conscious of their rage, then the responsibility extends to giving it form and shape. Rilke expressed this so well in a requiem written for a young poet who gave in to his tortured feelings and committed suicide.

> O ancient curse of poets!
> Being sorry for themselves instead of saying,
> for ever passing judgment on their feeling
> instead of shaping it, for ever thinking
> that what is sad or joyful in themselves
> is what they know and what in poems may fitly
> be mourned or celebrated. Invalids,
> using a language full of woefulness
> to tell us where it hurts, instead of sternly
> transforming into words those selves of theirs,
> as imperturbable cathedral carvers
> transposed themselves into the constant stone.
> That would have been salvation. Had you once
> perceived how fate may pass into a verse
> and not come back, how, once in, it turns image,
> nothing but image, but an ancestor
> who sometimes, when you watch him in his frame,
> seems to be like you and again not like you:—
> you would have persevered.[4]

The myth of Psyche and Amor suggests a way to gain access to rage and to transform it. In the myth, Psyche has lost her relation to Eros, her lover, and is trying to recover it by performing some tasks given to her by Eros' jealous mother, Aphrodite. The tasks seem impossible, and Psyche falls into despair. One task requires that she bring back golden fleece from some wild rams. Believing the task is impossible to complete, in hopelessness she goes to the river to drown herself. But then she hears a melodious voice which tells her there is a way to get the fleece from the raging rams. The voice comes from a kind, simple-hearted green reed in the water, a nurse of sweet music, who says:

> Psyche, racked though thou are by so many a woe, pollute not my sacred waters by slaying thyself thus miserably, nor at this hour approach those terrible sheep. For they borrow fierce heat from the blazing sun and wild frenzy maddens them, so that with sharp horns and foreheads hard as stone, and sometimes even with venomous bites, they vent their fury in the destruction of men. But till the heat of the noonday sun has assuaged its burning, and the beasts are lulled to sleep by the soft river breeze, thou canst hide thee beneath yonder lofty plane tree, which drinks of the river water even as I. And, when once the sheep have abated their madness and allayed their anger, go shake the leaves of yonder grove, and thou shalt find the golden wool clinging here and there to crooked twigs.[5]

Here the secret is not to approach the raging rams directly, for their rage is wild, crazy, and murderously destructive. The way to get access to all that energy is to wait patiently and approach it indirectly. To confront the raging power of the rams directly would mean Psyche's death and destruction. Sometimes because of her deep wounds, a woman's rage is so explosive that it shatters all her relationships. Like the frenzied rams, it charges aggressively at anyone in its path. Such rage is often rooted in feelings of abandonment, betrayal, and rejection which may go back to the relation with the father, and which often come up over and over again in current relationships. The rage is often mixed with feelings of jealousy and revenge that are strong enough to kill any relationship and the woman's capacity for loving herself as well. An extreme example in Greek tragedy is Medea, who was betrayed by her lover, Jason, and, in revenge, killed her own children. Many women destroy their relationships this way through continual hysterical outbursts or suicidal threats and attempts. Psyche's tendency toward suicide shows her possession by this deadly aggression which turned against her inwardly.

When Psyche waits until she can gather the golden fleece of the rams without being destroyed by their raging energy, she gains access to their creative golden energy, but without being destroyed in the process. To form the raging energy, it is necessary to gain access to it in its nondestructive aspect so that one does not become possessed by it. To do this takes patience and knowledge, i.e., waiting until the right time and knowing when that is. If one gets possessed by rage and explodes at the wrong time, the energy is usually wasted and often produces the opposite effect. All the other person or group sees is a wild reaction and not what is behind it. Knowing what is behind the rage is very important. And this takes conscious differentiation—differentiating from the experience of the rage and differentiating the various elements of the rage. That takes sorting out what part of the rage is the unsolved anger of the father, and what belongs to the woman herself and to the situation. The first task Psyche was asked to perform was sorting a giant pile of seeds into their different varieties. The pile was so enormous it seemed impossible. But some worker ants came along and helped Psyche do the job. Sometimes the job of sorting out the different elements of rage is enormous, too, and it takes a lot of work and determination. To sort out what part of the rage really belongs to you and how much is the other person's, or the unsolved rage of the parent, or even the rage of the culture is an enormous task. But if it is not done, then one frequently ends up in the hellish position of the Danaides in the ancient Greek story.

The Danaides were fifty daughters whose father finally agreed to their marriage to fifty male cousins. But he gave each daughter a sword so that on the wedding night, she could slay her husband. Forty-nine of the daughters used the sword to murder their husbands and were then condemned to Hell where they had continuously to fill a bottomless bowl with water. Since the bowl could never be filled, their task was impossible and endless. The fiftieth daughter, feeling sympathy for her new husband, helped him escape, and she was not sentenced to Hell. To act out the father's unsolved rage is to be like the Danaidean daughters who are promised by the father to the unwelcome suitors, then kill them with their father's rage, and ultimately are condemned to a hellish and futile existence. On the personal level, this might happen if a woman is possessed with unresolved anger, coming from the relationship to the father, and turns it inward, perhaps via suicide or other self-destructive behavior, thus killing off all chance for relationship. On the cultural level, the unsolved patriarchal rage against the feminine could be re-enacted by women who haven't found their own way to value their femininity, and so, by imitating the masculine or adapting to it, they end up never being able to form femininity.

Part of the forming is being able to contain what is to be formed, and this is actually the third task Psyche is given. It is also that which the Danaidean daughters were unable to do. Psyche's third task, after she has collected the fleece from the rams, is to fill a crystal bowl with the waters of a spring which feeds the rivers of the underworld. The spring flows from the highest crag of a rocky mountain guarded by dragons, and its voices tell Psyche to beware, that she cannot do it. But a noble eagle sent by Zeus takes the crystal urn and, soaring upward, cleverly fills the bowl with water. Containing some water from the stream that unites highest (mountain top) and lowest (underworld) is to be able to receive the flowing energy of life, uniting unconscious and conscious, and to give it some form. This requires the power to soar upwards, the power to show one's creative energy in the world without falling prey to the voices that say "beware, you cannot do it." Containing the energy and forming it means not dissipating it in formless rage but asserting it creatively. And this might happen in a political act, a work of art, raising a child, relating, and most of all in being, in the quality of one's life.

The following poem, "Apotheosis," expresses the transformation of rage.

> No pain
> nor other feeling
> just cresting
> on the pulse
> a certainty
> that all this
> is one
> that the old rage
> is love and power
> and yet drained[6]

Ultimately, the transformation of rage results in a strong
woman who with her creative energy and feminine wisdom
can contribute to the growth of herself, others, and the
culture. The acceptance and transformation of rage can
release and reveal feminine strength and spirit which can
redeem the wounded woman and ultimately the wound in the
father-daughter relationship as well.

CHAPTER SEVEN

TEARS

There is a palace that opens only to tears.
Zohar

Tears belong to the wounded woman. The tears can be congealed in icy form with the dagger-like points and edges of icicles. Or they may rush out in a torrential storm that can flood the ground upon which a woman stands. But the tears may also fall like the fructifying rain which enables growth and spring's rebirth.

When tears congeal into dagger-like icicles, they freeze up the woman and her relationships. Like Medusa's stare, these frozen tears can turn a man into stone; and the woman's heart can turn to stone as well. Tears in this form are not redemptive because the growth of the soul is frozen in bitter resentment.

Flooding tears, on the other hand, wash out the ground from under the woman. And in this muddied earth she can get stuck, unable to move and to stand on her own. Flooding tears can drown the wounded woman in a morass of sorrow that may turn into self-pity and deluge the soul.

Although frozen tears and flooding tears ultimately may not be redemptive, as tears they tear apart and open the soul. Along with rage, tears can release a woman and take part in healing and living with the wound.

A wounded relation with the father often obstructs a woman's relation to tears. Some fathers, who are afraid of their own tears, don't allow tears in their wives or daughters. A frequent dream theme I have found among women is when the father sells the daughter's tears. One way a father can sell his daughter's tears is to keep up a pleasant persona, encouraging his children to be cheerful and optimistic. Crying is then considered to be a sign of defeat and weakness. Other fathers may forbid tears through an emphasis on discipline and work. And fathers who drown in their own alcohol-laden tears are likely to cause their daughters to fear tears.

The following dream provides an example of the power of tears.

I had to stand in for another woman in a musical performance. I was to accompany a friend playing the guitar and singing. I didn't know the songs but I felt confident that I would be able to improvise. A little man approached me backstage before I was to go on. He was totally without expression through the entire dream. He kept trying to give me red wine to drink because if I spilled it on myself I would be in his power. I drank white wine and Perrier and felt I could avoid him. Then my son was there, and the man said that if my son cut himself and bled, he would be in the man's power. I told my son to be careful, but the man turned into a kitten. At first I told my son not to touch the kitten, but then I thought it's just a cute little kitten. My son played with the kitten and it scratched him. Then the kitten turned back into the man who said, "Your son is mine!" I got angry and when my husband arrived, I said, "That's not true, is it?" But my husband thought the man had won. Some time passed, perhaps I even woke up, and then I was crying, and the spell over my son was broken. Tears broke the spell!

This dream was one of a series of "path of water" dreams in which water was redemptive for this woman. Previously, she had a dream that she was being pursued by a salt man whom she felt symbolized her dried up tears and her tendency to

137

become possessed by a very demanding and pushy, inner masculine side. Her father had left home when she was ten. He never wrote or sent presents, although she wrote to him at Christmas and his birthday. Basically he ignored her, and she tried to make excuses for him in her mind. As she reached adolescence, she became rebellious and pursued a misfit mode of existence. She got into drugs and once, while hitch-hiking, was terrorized and almost murdered by a man who picked her up. She was gutsy and strong and from misfit she turned into fighter. Since she was extremely intuitive and highly articulate as well, she tended to tell people what was wrong with them and what to do about it. Often she was right, but because she was out of touch with her own vulnerability and the feeling that would give her a gentle way and good timing, she often hurt other people's feelings. And because others thought she was so tough and strong, they expected her to be able to take anything, and so she was frequently criticized and her vulnerability was overlooked. She resented this treatment, but was unable to express her suffering and her own needs.

Inwardly, she was tyrannized by a demanding inner man who expected continual perfection and striving, and who allowed her no rest. This inner man's demands were so extreme, requiring so much, that she was unable to actualize her talents because she couldn't live up to his superhuman ideals. She remembered her father had been demanding and perfectionistic: nothing was good enough, either to please him or to win him back home. And now she seemed to be possessed with the same hard perfectionism symbolized in the dream by the devilish man with the blank expression who wanted her under his spell. But the way to break his spell was through tears. This meant to allow her feelings to be and to let them show rather than to cover them up with a hard exterior. It meant to be easier on others and to be easier on herself—on her self-expectation and on her feminine bodily needs as well. It also meant to accept her wounds and the power of the devil. She felt that spilling the red wine on herself would have acknowledged her imperfection and humiliation. In the dream she avoided that, but could not avoid her son's bleeding. She felt she had to acknowledge the bleeding wound and the power this man had over her before the spell could be broken. And her tears were a concrete acknowledgement of her wound.

In therapy the breakthrough for many women comes when they can simply let down and cry, living out their vulnerability and wounds. Quite often they feel ashamed and humiliated when they cry. And yet their crying often turns out to be both helpful and hopeful, for it breaks through their defenses and acknowledges their wounds—the wounds that must be entered and accepted before healing can occur. As one woman expressed it: "Crying and not knowing why was a great relief. Before I thought I always had to have an answer or an explanation. Being able to cry in therapy with a caring person present allowed me to fully acknowledge my pain, to feel my wound."

Another woman dreamt she was in a terrifying rainstorm that threatened to flood her car and keep it from moving. Yet when she looked at the stormy sky, a translucent light was shining. Behind the storm of her uncontrollable feelings was the light that would enable her to have a new vision. This woman had lived her life primarily as a dutiful daughter, serving others. Her mother was crippled, and she had to care for her. The mother cried in pain, while the daughter tried to comfort. Physically, her father was partly deaf, and, psychologically, he turned away from both his wife and daughter. He did not hear their cries. And her grandmother was a severe, moralistic judge, denying the value of feelings. The daughter was denied emotional and physical care and comfort by all three adults in her family. Her own feelings were not allowed and cherished. Instead she became the caretaker and as a child lived a life of service, eventually entering a convent where she remained for the first twenty years of her adult life. Although she developed her spiritual and intellectual sides, her emotional and sexual life was denied. After she left the convent, she sought desperately for an intimate relationship. But her pattern was to help others, trying to please them and win their affections. If they did not respond to her on the level of physical and emotional intimacy, she felt hurt and used. All the years of denied crying over her unlived childhood and over her loss of emotional and physical intimacy needed to come out. She needed to accept and experience the storm of her unlived life before she could move on. She needed to express her own pain. And, as the dream revealed, these stormy feelings were her guiding light.

The image of rain as redemptive, symbolizing the tears of transformation, comes up in many women's dreams. And it is a frequent image in the poet's vision. Rilke ends his great poetic work, *Duino Elegies*, with this image of rain. *Duino Elegies* expresses the lament of human existence. "Who, if I cried, would hear me among the angelic orders?...And so I keep down my heart, and swallow the call-note of depth-dark sobbing."[1] Throughout the ten elegies Rilke gives expression to the wound in human existence, to the despair, alienation, and hopelessness felt by all wounded persons, men and women alike, as they experience their transitoriness, their fears, their divided nature, their inability to be perfect and to possess what they want, the travesties of injustice and war in their personal and cultural histories, and finally the fact of impending death. Rilke was himself in despair when he began the *Duino Elegies*. It took him ten years to complete this poetic cycle. In the course of his ten years of writing, he raged and he wept. But finally he was given a vision of the meaning in all this suffering. Finally he was able to emerge from lament to praise in the realization that sorrows themselves are part of our growth, a necessary season and place in the course of our development. Rilke realized that the source of both sorrow and joy was the same "carrying stream," just as life and death are sides of one whole realm. And so, though we tend to think of pain, depression, and other falling moments as something to be avoided, and we associate happiness with rising moods and successes, ultimately they belong together. Rain is an image of this cycle of growth. As Rilke expresses it when he ends the *Duino Elegies* in a spirit of hope and affirmation:

And yet, were they waking a likeness within us, the endlessly dead, look, they'd be pointing, perhaps to the catkins, hanging from empty hazels, or else they'd be meaning the rain that falls on the dark earth in the early spring. And we, who have always thought of happiness climbing, would feel the emotion that almost startles when happiness falls.[2]

Redemption via tears occurs in the Grimm Brothers' fairy tale "The Handless Maiden."[3] This fairy tale also portrays the father-daughter wound. In it, a poor, unemployed miller meets in the forest a man who promises unlimited wealth to the miller if he will give the man whatever stands behind his mill. Thinking he has nothing of value and that only an apple tree stands there, the miller agrees. But as it turns out, his daughter was standing there, and the man in the forest is really the devil. So the father turns his daughter over to the devil, a thing which wounded fathers often do. This father makes the bet because he thinks he has nothing of value, nothing to lose, and, hence, there is no real sacrifice on his part. But he forgets he has a daughter who is of value, and in this forgetting he undervalues his daughter and himself as father.

The daughter, upon hearing this transaction, washes herself clean to keep out of the devil's hands. The devil says she must be kept away from all water, otherwise he has no power over her. The father obeys the devil, but in the meantime the daughter weeps, and the tears fall upon her hands. Since the devil cannot take someone who has so wept, he tells the father to cut off his daughter's hands and he will come back for her the next day. Otherwise, the devil threatens to take the father. In terror for his own life, the father cuts off his daughter's hands. But the daughter weeps again and the tears fall on her arms. Once more the devil cannot take her. So the devil doesn't get the girl, and the daughter is now handless. The father tries to make amends to his handless daughter, saying they can live securely with the new fortune. But seeing the situation clearly, the daughter refuses to stay with her father. Instead she goes off into the forest alone.

Here is a daughter who sees her father's weakness and realizes she must go on her own. But her handlessness means that she cannot go the way of ego-activity as compensation. Her weeping saves her from the devil and separates her from the negligent father. And it results in going her own way into the virgin forest where she prays for divine help and trusts the healing forces of nature. An angel comes to help her and she feeds from the fruit of a tree belonging to a king who falls in love with her, marries her, and gives her silver hands. But then the two are separated by war when the king must go and fight. The devil intercedes with false messages and the girl is again required to go off on her own with her newly born son, called *Schmerzenreich* (rich in sorrows). Again the girl prays for help and an angel offers her a home in the forest where she stays for seven years. During this seven year period of waiting in the forest, her hands grow back naturally. Meanwhile the king searches for her these seven long years and, finally, through a combination of patience and accepted suffering, the two are reunited.

For me this fairy tale was very meaningful at a time when I was aware of the danger and defense of my Amazon armor. I realized that all my ego attempts for super-achievement and control, to compensate my father's weaknesses, ultimately were of no avail. Suddenly handless, I had to wait in the forest of my loneliness and depression, and learn to wait and trust. During this period my tears continued to fall. Sometimes I would return to bitter resentment about my unlived childhood and the abandonment by my father and various of my lovers, and then the tears would harden into aggressive icicles. Other times, the flooding tears would come, and then I would begin to drown as a victim. But along with these tears came the softer ones that opened me up to my spontaneous instinctual feelings—feelings that had long been repressed and suppressed. As my tears softened my armor and opened up my heart, I began to feel nature's healing power. More and more I could express my vulnerability and not try to justify myself by the accepted collective means. The more openly and spontaneously I began to show my feelings to others, the more my anxiety and control defenses disappeared, and the more others opened up to me. I began to realize that my suffering, my open wound, was one of the most important links I had to people. It was not in doing something special that my redemption lay. It was by accepting the healing forces of nature and learning to wait and be open to what comes up spontaneously from the depths. For me, a super-achiever, this was not easy. Yet, as the tears fell upon me over and over again—even to the end of writing my book—my hands began to grow back naturally. And finally I could begin to write and talk out of my center.

In some ways I see this to be the meaning of Psyche's failure at the end of her fourth task when, after all her work of performing each task, she succumbs to taking the forbidden beauty potion and falls unconscious and helpless. Psyche has been performing these tasks to regain her relation to her lover, Eros. Neumann says that by taking the forbidden beauty potion, she acknowledges the greater power of masculine Eros, and by preferring beauty to knowledge she reunites with the feminine in her nature.[4] Many women in our time feel offended by the assumption that the feminine is primarily beauty. I see Neumann's interpretation echoing the split between puella and Amazon, reducing the feminine to the beautiful one. When I look at Psyche's "failure" as an aspect of transformation, I see her giving up as a surrender to the greater powers of the psyche, an admission of her human frailty and limitation. This acknowledgment is necessary for all human beings, not only for women, though its value is often first revealed by the feminine.

In the same way, fructifying tears are often interpreted as failure. But they soften the ground for new growth and protect one from possession by devilish and revengeful activity and from drowning in helpless passivity. The active waiting and acceptance of suffering that the Handless Maiden's tears bring save her from both puella passivity and armored control, and allow her the active receptivity of faith, hope, and trustful confidence that lead to healing. They are tears of transformation. Here is an image for the wounded woman. First comes all the pain and rage against the wound. Then, with acceptance of the wound come the tears of transformation and a natural healing that can lead to love and compassion.

III.

THE HEALING

Someday, emerging at last from this terrifying vision,
may I burst into jubilant praise to assenting Angels!
May not even one of the clear-struck keys of the heart
fail to respond through alighting on slack or doubtful
or rending strings! May a new-found splendour appear
in my streaming face! My inconspicuous Weeping
flower! How dear you will be to me then, you Nights
of Affliction! Oh, why did I not, inconsolable sisters,
more bendingly kneel to receive you, more loosely surrender
myself to your loosened hair? We wasters of sorrows!
How we stare away into sad endurance beyond them,
trying to foresee their end! Whereas they are nothing else
than our winter foliage, our sombre evergreen, one
of the seasons of our interior year,—not only
season—they're also place, settlement, camp, soil, dwelling.

Rainer Maria Rilke
Duino Elegies

CHAPTER EIGHT
FEMININE FACETS

Daily, hourly we must keep the crystal clear that
the colours may assume their order. I pray to fulfill
my task, don't elude me now for my soul's sake.
I must live so that clarity produces the order of
diversity. Nothing less than bearing it all will
do, for it is the creation of a change of consciousness.
                                    Florida Scott-Maxwell

After describing the different lifestyles of the eternal girl
and the armored Amazon, I realized that I had experienced
all of them at different times in my life, and that each of these
modes of existence has its own constructive side as well as its
limiting aspects. It also occurred to me that each has
something to contribute to the other.

The image that comes to me is a crystal. A crystal has
different facets and when turned towards the sun in different
ways, it reveals unique forms of brilliance. It is the same with
a woman. By turning the crystal of the Self, she can have
access to the appropriate quality at the right moment.

The darling doll, for example, has the strength of being
able to receive from others. Many women are cut off from
emotionally rich lives because they are afraid to receive what
others have to give them. The darling doll can give by
receiving, and she can adapt and accommodate herself to the

other, thus enabling dialogue in the relationship. She is also able to adapt to the collective, thus enabling her to be a contributing member of the society in which she lives. When she cuts herself off from her own identity by adapting to what the other wants, that is when she suffers a loss of relationship to the Self.

The girl of glass has a different strength. Hers is a sensitive connection to the inner life and the realm of fantasy and imagination. Although she may be afraid of the outer world, in the inner world she is as adventurous as any hero. With this capacity she can both inspire creativity in others and be creative herself if she does not give in to her tendency to retreat from life.

The high flyer's quest for challenge and adventure is a strength that leads to change and exploration of new possibilities. She has the audacity to try new things, to explore the unknown. If she doesn't lose herself in dispersion through her tendency not to stay with one thing, she can be a model for change and exploration in our society.

The misfit's strength lies in her ability to question the established collective values. Because she tends to live out the shadow, i.e., the unaccepted side of society, she has a connection with just those qualities that are needed, yet rejected by the culture. If she can overcome her tendency to be a victim and an alienated outsider, she can be one of the major forces that transform society.

Just as each puella lifestyle has its special contribution to the whole woman, so does each Amazon lifestyle have its own special quality that strengthens a woman's development. The superstar, with her discipline and ability to achieve, shows to the world the strength and competence of women. If these capacities come out of her feminine center rather than an armored ego defense, she will enjoy the fruits of her work and creativity, and society will be enhanced by her contributions.

The dutiful daughter's capacity to be responsible and to endure despite difficulty is an essential quality for the stability of life, work, and relationship. Her positive relation to obedience and sense of law and order is necessary for functioning well in any society, organization, or relationship. If the duty and obedience comes from a grounded center and does not alienate her from her spontaneous feeling, she can contribute the endurance and commitment needed for the actualization of feminine creativity.

The martyr's tendency to give and sacrifice is essential for creative life and relationship. Historically, the martyrs have been a model for female heroism, e.g., Joan of Arc. But the sacrifice must not be at the expense of the feminine Self. If the martyr can learn to enjoy and give to herself, then her capacity to give and sacrifice for others will no longer be self-denying or guilt-provoking, but a source of inspiration.

The warrior queen is in touch with her anger and assertion. She knows how to fight to survive and she can take care of herself. This is a quality needed by everyone, but especially in our time by women. The alienation for the warrior queen occurs when she forgets her feminine feeling and softness and her fighting turns into a machine-gun-like attack. If the warrior queen can rest in her feminine center and be assertive when appropriate, she can show the way to develop feminine strength and power in individual women's lives and in our culture.

Each of these modes of existence has something to offer the others. Gloria, who lived primarily as a darling doll, learned to use the warrior queen's assertiveness to stand up to others' demands and the high flyer's spirit of adventure to try new things. She used the misfit's ability to say no to collective standards that were enslaving her. The girl of glass taught her a better relation to her inner self, while the superstar encouraged her to show her abilities to the world.

Grace was a girl of glass. She needed to fly high with confidence and show her inner values out in the world like the high flyer and the superstar, so that she could contribute to society her special relation to fantasy and the life of the soul. When she allowed herself to be adored like the darling doll, she opened to the love and admiration she deserved. From the misfit she learned to be herself no matter what society might judge. And the warrior queen gave her the strength to assert

149

herself. The dutiful daughter's endurance provided her with the stability to actualize her fantasies. And the martyr gave her the sense of heroic self-justification she needed.

Juanita, the high flyer, actualized her wildest intuitions and daring relation to possibility by combining the dutiful daughter's responsibility, the warrior queen's consistent strength, and the martyr's ability to sacrifice. Through knowing the girl of glass, she deepened her relation to her feminine soul. Appreciating the darling doll enabled her to value commitment to a partner.

In some ways, the misfit seems to be the most difficult of the puella ways of existence. Yet by virtue of her dis-relationsip to society, she questions it and thus can change it with the help of the strength of the warrior queen, the endurance of the dutiful daughter, and the martyr's ability to sacrifice. Jean was such a woman. She took from the darling doll a more accepting relationship to the collective so that she could relate to society enough to change it. In the high flyer she found an optimistic relation to possibility that enabled her to rise above the cynical pessimism that victimized her. And the girl of glass gave her the sensitive care for her soul that allowed her to be tender to herself and others.

Since the superstar tends to be constantly striving in the outer world, Pat needed the ability to retreat and rest in that inner space so natural to the girl of glass. She also needed to be able to receive like the darling doll, to defy society's demands for performance as the misfit could, and to soar like the high flyer above the demands for achievement. In general, I have found the Amazon lifestyles to be closer to each other than the puella modes. So quite often the super-star is able to be dutiful, sacrificial, and to fight. But if she can accept these qualities as more important than her need to achieve, then they can give her a strength greater than ego ambition.

Constance, a dutiful daughter, did not know how to let go and enjoy herself. Acting out some of her fantasies the way the high flyer would and rebelling at times like the misfit were effective in counteracting her rigid obedience. She needed the darling doll's ability to be adored for her playful qualities rather than for her efficiency. And the girl of glass showed her how to turn her submission to others into a sensitive commitment to the needs of her inner soul. The dutiful daughter tends to be bound to society, so the warrior queen's assertiveness helped Constance counteract her tendency to put society's needs over her own.

Mary had the martyr's tendency toward self-denial. When she learned the darling doll's ability to receive affection, the high flyer's capacity to have fun and adventure, and the misfit's spirit of rebellion, she was able to shrug off the heavy burdens she had been carrying so stoically. The pleasures of the inner life were opened by the girl of glass's relation to fantasy. Since she tended to deny her own aggression and protect it by making others feel guilty for her sacrifices, she needed to acknowledge her assertiveness the way the warrior queen does. The superstar's ability to receive the fruits of her achievements countered Mary's tendency to deny herself all fruits of her activity.

Jackie had the warrior queen's hard, aggressive stance and needed some of the softness and receptivity of the darling doll in order to be able to receive love. The sensitivity of the girl of glass opened her to her inner life, and the high flyer's zest countered her seriousness. From the misfit's rebellion against the collective values she learned to fight for her own unique values. As a fighter, Jackie had the endurance of the dutiful daughter, and the superstar's capacity to achieve, but she needed their less strident manner. And from the martyr who sacrifices ego wishes to a greater cause, the fighter experiences the positive side of the death of the ego in favor of the greater feminine self.

Finding a relationship to the various feminine facets one has within is part of a woman's journey towards being a whole person. It is also a healing process. For me, healing is like a long journey. Recently I took a springtime hike in the Rockies with a dear friend. We started out in the warm sun and admired how beautiful were the aspens trembling with new buds. But then came the long and strenuous hike. Passing through a goblin-like forest, we emerged into the high altitude—overcome with both the grandeur of space and also the dizzying panic of the high altitude. Next came some climbs over snow fields and rocks. Finally we emerged to a circular place where lake, mountain, and sky were so dramatically united that just being there was both terrifying and beautiful. It was as Rilke expressed it: "Beauty's just the beginning of terror." We had hiked for hours through many terrains and ascending levels of altitudes. And just as we arrived at the mystical lake, surrounded by mountainous grandeur on all sides, a storm arrived. The sun departed, the clouds surrounded, the hail descended, and suddenly it felt as though we were in danger for our lives.

We had walked for hours to this place; climbed over rocks and snow; and once there we knew it was a holy place. But we could only stay a short time if we were to return home safely. So back again we went through the snow fields and rocks, on alpine tundra, back through the goblin forest and finally to our shimmering aspens. Making our way even through the hail and rain, we returned home at last. And yet, even in the moment when we reached our beginning point, we knew we would return to take this journey again. We also knew that the journey would be different next time.

Journeying through the terrain of the feminine facets has the same quality for me. Some of the trails are easy and pleasant, like that lined with the fragile beauty of the shimmering aspens. Some lead through the enchanted forest of the goblins. And some require the struggle of climbing the rocks, slipping on the snow, and not succumbing to vertigo. To arrive at the mystical lake, to be at the crystal of the self, requires all.

It is the same, I believe, with the feminine quest for wholeness. No aspect can be left out. One woman will find one route appealing. Another woman may enjoy a different way. Yet ultimately we need to go through all terrains. Men's journey toward wholeness requires a similar encounter with all terrains. But here I speak of the feminine route since it is the one I know best and the one that has been in the background culturally.

Like the crystal, the journey through the various feminine facets is another image for finding feminine wholeness. It stresses the various joys and sufferings along the way—the wounding, the hurting, the healing, the struggle, the vitality, and the continual return.

Turning the crystal of the feminine self to allow these different qualities to shine forth in their strength rather than their weakness is a challenge that women face today. And the integration of these many facets can be the foundation for finding the feminine spirit.

CHAPTER NINE

REDEEMING THE FATHER

If we expect from men that they turn
to their invisible inner feminine
qualities, then it would seem natural
that women should give an example and
show the men in their own lives what
"femininity" could mean.

Hilde Binswanger

"Where are the myths and stories of feminine quests and courage?" is a question I frequently hear women ask. Where are some models for feminine development? One story that helped me in my own quest is a fairy tale about a courageous girl who goes off in search of medicine that can heal her blind and sick father. Through her journey she enables her father to see again and to value the feminine. And it results in her marriage to a man who has admired her cleverness, courage, and kindness, all qualities which have enabled her to accomplish this act of redemption. The fairy tale is from the land of Tadzhikistan which borders on Afghanistan in the south and on China in the east, a land whose culture and language are akin to Persia. The fairy tale is entitled "The Courageous Girl."[1]

An old man who longs for a son but instead has three daughters falls ill and becomes blind. In a faraway land there is a surgeon who has medicine that can heal blindness, and the father laments that he has no sons to get the healing medicine, believing this task to be impossible for the daughters. But after the eldest daughter entreats him to let her try, he agrees. Dressed in man's clothing for the journey, she sets off and encounters a sick old woman and gives her some food. The old woman says it is impossible to get the medicine, for all brave lads who have tried have perished. Upon hearing this, the eldest daughter loses all hope and goes back home. Then the second daughter wants to try, and although the father discourages her, she sets out on the journey, also dressed in man's clothing. She too encounters the sick old woman, giving her something to eat, and the old woman tells her it is very difficult to reach this goal and that she will perish in vain. So the second daughter loses courage and goes back home. Whereupon the father sighs heavily, "Ah, how pitiful is a man who has no sons!"

The youngest daughter's heart is struck by these words and she implores her father to let her go. At first the father tells her it is better to stay at home than venture forth in vain, but finally he accedes once more. So the youngest daughter puts on men's clothing and sets off on the journey to get the healing medicine. When she encounters the old woman, she greets her politely, helps her wash, and gladly feeds her. The old woman is impressed with the tender and pleasant way of this youth but says that it is better to stay with her or return home, since such a tender lad will not succeed when so many tall, strong men already have failed. But the girl refuses to turn back. And because of the kindness and courage of this youth, the old woman reveals how to get the medicine.

The surgeon who has the medicine requires the seeds of a tree whose fruit has great healing power. But this tree is in the possession of the Dev, a three-headed evil monster. To reach the tree, the girl must perform some kind acts toward his animals and servants and then take a fruit while the Dev is asleep. And for protection against the Dev, in case he should come after her, the old woman gives her a mirror, a comb, and a whetstone to throw backwards over her shoulder

155

to stop the Dev from following her. When the youngest daughter reaches the Dev's dwelling, she sees that the gate is dirty and warped, and so she quickly cleans it and hangs it straight. Inside, she sees some huge dogs and horses chained against different walls, but the hay is in front of the dogs and the bones in front of the horses. She puts the hay by the horses and the bones by the dogs and goes on. Then she meets some servant girls whose bare arms are burnt because they have to reach inside a red hot oven to bake food for the Dev. She befriends the servant girls and sews a protective sleeve for each one. Grateful, they tell her that the tree has no fruit, but that a sack of seeds from the tree is under the Dev's pillow. If all his eyes are open, it means he is asleep and she can take the seeds. The girl finds the Dev asleep and takes the seeds, but the Dev awakens and shouts to the servant girls and the dogs and horses to catch the thief and tells the gate to shut. Because the girl has helped them, they all refuse to obey, and so the Dev sets out himself to pursue the girl. She throws over her shoulder the mirror which turns into a swift river and this stops the Dev for a while. But soon he catches up with her, so she flings back the whetstone which turns into a mountain, barring the Dev's path. When once again he catches up, she throws the comb back over her shoulder and that turns into a gigantic dense forest, too great for the Dev to penetrate, so he gives up the chase and returns home.

Finally the girl reaches the surgeon's house. Since she has the seeds and since she has been "a daring and courageous young man," he gives her the medicine to heal her father's eyes and half of the healing seeds as well. The girl thanks him from the bottom of her heart, and the surgeon invites her to remain a few days as his guest. However, one of the surgeon's friends suspects her true identity, that she is a girl in disguise. The surgeon can't believe that such a daring, courageous hero who has done this most precious deed could be a girl, so the friend suggests the following test: to put white chrysanthemums under the pillows of both the surgeon's son and the girl, who are staying in the same room. If the daring hero is a girl, the flowers will wither, says the friend, but if the hero is a young man, the flowers will stay fresh. The girl, guessing this scheme, stays awake all night and just before dawn finds the withered flowers under her pillow and replaces them with fresh ones from the garden. So when the surgeon finds the flowers in the morning, both bunches are fresh. But the surgeon's son has been awake during the night and has seen everything the visitor has done, and, full of curiosity, decides to escort this visitor home.

By the time the girl gets home, her father has become totally bedridden in his grief and rues the day he let his daughter try to get the medicine for him. But when the youngest daughter brings the medicine to her father, he soon is cured of his blindness and all his other ills. After she tells about all the adventures she has gone through to procure the healing medicine, her father weeps in joy, saying he will never again regret not having a son, for his daughter has shown the devotion of ten sons and has healed him. The surgeon's son, seeing that his companion is a girl and not a boy, declares his love for her and asks for her hand in marriage. And when the daughter says there is a deep bond of friendship between them, her father is full of joy. Thus, the fearless and clever maiden and the son of the learned surgeon marry and live happily ever after.

This fairy tale describes a father who is sick and blind, who cannot see the total value of the feminine. Although he loves his daughters dearly, he does not believe they are able to go out in the world and get the medicine to heal him. The only representative of the feminine spirit is a sick old woman who knows how to get the medicine but who believes the task is impossible, even for men. The three daughters want to try. Here is an image of a wounded father, injured in his relation to the feminine, yet only the feminine can save him—the old woman has the knowledge and the daughters have the spunk and motivation.

The daughters have to dress in men's clothing to set out on the journey, and this shows the low estimation and mistrust of the feminine. To show themselves as women would most likely result in immediate defeat. The first phase of feminine liberation in our culture also required that women act like men to succeed in the world. Women were not accepted by either men or women in terms of their own feminine contributions in most professions. Although the first two daughters give up and return home, nevertheless there is some progress made. They all are ready to go out in the world and try. And although the old woman tells the first daughter the task is "impossible," after that encounter, she changes and tells the second daughter the task is very "difficult." And by the time the third daughter comes, although the old woman at first tries to dissuade her, she finally does share the knowledge needed to complete the task. As the daughters keep on trying, the older woman becomes more optimistic and finally communicates her knowledge and wisdom. This corresponds symbolically to the gradual progress made by women in their united efforts to be recognized and gain their rights. Although the youngest daughter is still disguised as a man when the old woman tells her how to get the healing medicine, she has impressed the woman through the combination of her tender kindness and plucky courage—two qualities often thought of as opposing, the former ascribed by culture to women and the latter to men. In combining them, the youngest daughter shows the possibility to integrate them. And it is via this integration that she learns how to gain access to the healing power.

The tree with the fruit that heals is in the possession of the Dev, a raging monster. The youngest daughter has to face the rage and the power of this destructive masculine figure in order to gain access to the healing power. Redemption of the father invariably seems to require facing monstrous rage and aggression, both one's own and that which the father himself was unable to integrate. On the cultural level, confronting rage vis-a-vis the patriarchal fathers has been necessary to make feminine needs and value known. The way the daughter wrests the healing seeds from the angry monster, however, is not through a head-on attack. She is considerate, kind, and helpful; she oils the gate (the entryway), feeds the animals (instincts), and protects the burned arms of the servant girls (the feminine)—all aspects the monster has neglected. And so because she has helped them, they come to the aid of the girl rather than the monster. These are also all aspects of the father-daughter relationship that need to be healed. The entryway between the daughter and the world has not been cared for, the feminine instincts are chained and not given the right food, and the feminine ability to handle the world (the arms) has been burnt by reducing women to the status of servants. In caring for these, the kind and courageous girl is able to get the healing seeds from the monster. But she still has to stop him in his attempt to get them back, as many women who have initially made important steps in their self-healing and growth may be attacked again by the old monstrous forces. That means they must continue to make the effort to keep their gained development and not fall back into old passive ways. To use against the monster's pursuit, the girl has the old woman's gifts—the mirror, whetstone, and comb. The mirror enables one to see oneself clearly in reflection, the whetstone is used for sharpening tools, and the comb to untangle and shape the hair which provides a frame to one's face and identity. When the feminine is so formed, these objects turn into natural forces which stop the attack of the monster.

Although the courageous girl has retrieved the healing seeds from the monster and gives them to the surgeon, who in turn gives her the medicine to heal her father's eyes, she has one test left before she can redeem the father. She now has a relation to the physician who heals, but she cannot yet reveal she is a girl. At a certain point in a woman's development and to achieve certain tasks, it is necessary to use her masculine side. Given the social conditions, the courageous girl had to keep her disguise as a boy to fool them so that ultimately the worth of her feminine being could be valued. If at this point the girl were to reveal she was not a man, it might interfere with the completion of the task—to heal the father. For it is precisely feminine courage and ability that the father and the culture have been unable to see. This is echoed in the doctor's disbelief that such a heroic act could have been

159

performed by a girl. Often women who are trying to gain access to their own strength and ability give up before they have gone all the way, sometimes by getting into a love relationship and projecting their newly gained strength and power back on the partner, thus losing it for themselves. This possibility is present for the courageous girl since the doctor's son is a potential partner. But she is alert to this danger. The fragility and transitoriness of the feminine strength is symbolized by the wilting flower, and the girl stays awake all night and provides a fresh flower, which is analogous to the consciousness and action required by women to show that their feminine strength and courage are not a transitory or passing event but something permanent. And the uniqueness of this action is observed by the doctor's son so that he is interested in getting to know this person better and decides to accompany her home. When the girl returns home with the medicine and her father is able to see again, he realizes he has devalued the power of his daughters and, weeping with joy, he is now able to see the value of the feminine, saying he will never again regret not having a son. The doctor's son, who had cherished a deep love for his new friend, after discovering she is a girl, asks to marry her. And when the girl tells of the deep bond of friendship between them, the father joyfully consents to the marriage. So after the girl redeems the father, who then sees the value of the feminine, the girl is freed to marry—a marriage based not on cultural projections about the feminine but on a deep and mutual bond of friendship and on the man's love and admiration for the woman's courage and knowledge. The redemption of the father, both on the personal and cultural levels, can lead to this potential—the mature union of masculine and feminine. And the girl, with this union, can act in her original feminine form showing all its strength and spirit!

Here is a fairy tale that provides an image of the way a daughter can heal the father's wound. And in the process the daughter gains a deep connection to her own strength and courage, to the power of her own feminine spirit, and to a loving relationship with the masculine. How might this process of redeeming the father be manifested on the personal and cultural levels?

On the personal level, the redemption may be possible only inwardly, for the actual father may be dead or not open to a new relationship. But that doesn't diminish the importance of this task. As the protagonist of the play *I Never Sang for My Father* says: "Death ends a life, but it doesn't end a relationship."[2] The relation to the inner father still needs to be transformed. Otherwise the old destructive patterns coming from the impaired relationship will continue. One part of this transformation process entails seeing the destructive patterns and how they have affected one's life. Another aspect entails seeing the value of the father, for if one doesn't relate to the positive side of the father, that aspect of the psyche remains cut off, unintegrated, and potentially destructive to one's life. On the cultural level, redemption of the father also requires seeing both the positive and negative aspects of the father. And it requires changing the cultural ruling principles so that both the feminine and masculine are uniquely valued and equally influential.

Redeeming the father has been for me the central issue of my personal and spiritual development. For the wounded relation to my father disturbed so many important areas in my life—my femininity, my relation to men, play, sexuality, creativity, and a confident way of being in the world. As a therapist, I have seen that finding a new relation to the father is an important issue for any woman with an impaired relation to the father. And culturally, I believe it is an issue for every woman, since the relation to the cultural ruling fathers needs to be transformed.

In my own life, redeeming the father has been a long process. It started when I went into Jungian analysis. With the help of a kind and supportive woman analyst who provided a warm, protective container for the emerging energies, I entered into a new realm—the symbolic world of dreams. There I encountered sides of myself I never knew existed. I also discovered my father there—the father I had long ago rejected. There was in myself, I discovered, not only the personal father I remembered. There were a variety of paternal figures, images of an archetypal Father. This father had more faces than I had ever imagined, and that realization was awesome. It terrified me and it also gave me hope. My ego-identity, my notions about who I was, crumbled. There was in me a power stronger than my consciously acknowledged self. This power rolled over my attempts to control my life and events around me, as an avalanche changes the face of a mountain. From then on, my life required that I learn to relate to this greater power.

In rejecting my father, I had been refusing my power, for the rejection of my father entailed refusing all of his positive qualities as well as the negative ones. So, along with the irresponsibility and irrational dimension that I had denied, I lost access to my creativity, spontaneity, and feminine feeling. My dreams kept pointing this out. One dream said that my father was very rich and owned a great palatial Tibetan temple. Another said he was a Spanish king. This contradicted the poor, degraded man I knew as "father." As far as my own powers went, my dreams showed that I was refusing them too. In one dream a magic dog gave me the power to make magic opals. I made the opals and had them in my hand, but then I gave them away and didn't keep any for myself. In another dream, a meditation teacher said, "You are beautiful but you don't recognize it." And a voice said to me in still another dream, "You have the key to medial knowledge and you must take it." But I woke up screaming in terror that I didn't want the responsibility. The irony was that although I criticized and hated my father for being so irresponsible and letting his potentialities go down the drain, I was doing the very same thing. I wasn't really valuing myself and what I had to offer. Instead I alternated between the unconfident, fragile pleasing puella and the dutiful, achieving armored Amazon.

Because of my rejection of my father, my life was split into a number of unintegrated and conflicting figures, each trying to keep control. Ultimately this leads to an explosive situation. For a long time I was unable to accept the death of these individual identities for the greater unknown unity that could ground my magic—the mysterious ground of my being, which I later found to be the source of healing. And so I experienced this powerful ground of my being in the form of anxiety attacks. Because I would not let go willingly and open up to the greater powers, they overwhelmed me and showed me their threatening face. They struck me suddenly and repeatedly in the core of my being, shocking me out of my controlling patterns like lightning jolts open a closed and clutching hand. Now I knew how little help my defenses really were. Suddenly I was face to face with the void. I wondered if this was what my father had experienced too, and whether his drinking was an attempt to ward this off. Perhaps "the spirits" of alcohol that ruled his being were a substitute for the greater spirits, and perhaps even a defense against them because they were so close. Since I had denied any value to my father after he "drowned" in the irrational Dionysian realm, I needed to learn to value that rejected area by letting go of the need to control. But this required experiencing the negative side, being plunged into the uncontrollable chaos of feelings and impulses, into the dark depths where the unknown treasure was hidden. Ultimately, to redeem the father required that I enter the underworld, that I value that rejected area in myself. And that led to honoring the spirits. Jungian analysis led me to this and writing has furthered this process.

Writing has been a way to redeem my father. As a child, I had always wanted to be a writer. Finally taking the risk to put my insights on paper required a lot of assertion and courage. The strength of a written word requires the writer to stand behind it. Writing required me to focus on and commit myself to the relationship with my father. I had to really look at him, to try to understand his side of the story, his aspirations and despair. No longer could I dismiss him from my life as though I could totally escape the past and his influence. Nor could I simply blame him as the cause of all my troubles. Now, through my writing, we were suddenly

163

face to face. Like Orual in *Till We Have Faces*, when I looked in the mirror I saw my father's face. This was incredibly painful because my father had carried the shadow side of my existence, all that was dark, terrifying, and bad. But strangely enough it was a source of light and hope as well, because in all that darkness shone the creative light of the underworld's imaginative powers. And I felt the force of its masculine energy as well. About a year after I started writing and really facing my father, I had the following dream:

> I saw some beautiful poppies, glowing with red, orange, and yellow colors and I wished my mother-analyst were there with me to see them. I went through the field of poppies and crossed a stream. Suddenly I was in the underworld at a banquet table with many men. Red wine was flowing and I decided to take another glass. As I did, the men raised their wine glasses in salute to my health, and I felt warm and glowing with their affectionate tribute.

The dream marked my initiation into the underworld. I had passed from the bright world of the mother into the realm of the dark father-lover. But there I was saluted as well. This was of course an incestuous situation and yet a necessary one for me. Part of the father's role, according to Kohut, is to let himself be idealized by the daughter and then gradually allow her to detect his realistic limitations without withdrawing from her.[3] And of course with the ideal projection goes deep love. In my own development the love turned to hate, so that the previous ideals associated with my father were rejected. I had to learn to love my father again so I could reconnect with his positive side. I had to learn to value my father's playful, spontaneous, magic side, but also to see its limits, as well as how the positive aspects could be actualized in my life. Loving the Father-ideal allowed me to love my own ideal and to realize that ideal in myself. This entailed first seeing my father's value and then realizing that that belonged to me. This broke the unconscious incestuous bond and freed me for my own relation to the transcendent powers in my Self.

For wounded daughters who are in poor relation to other sides of the father, the details of the redemption may be different, but the central issue will be the same. To redeem the father requires seeing the hidden value the father has to offer. For example, those daughters who have reacted against the too authoritarian father are likely to have problems accepting their own authority. Such women tend to adapt or react rebelliously. They need to see the value in their own responsibility, in accepting their own power and strength. They need to value limit, go up to it and see the edges, but know when too much is too much. They need to know when to say no and when to say yes. This means having realistic ideals and knowing their own limits and the limits of the situation. To put it in Freudian terms, they need to get a positive relation to the "super-ego," the inner voice of valuation and responsible judgment and decision-making. This voice, when it is constructive, is neither too critical and severe nor too indulgent, so that they can see and hear objectively what is there. One woman expressed it this way: "I need to hear the voice of the father inside tell me in a kind way when I'm doing a good job, but also when I'm off the mark." Redemption of this aspect of the father means the transformation of the critical judge, who proclaims one constantly "guilty," and the defense lawyer, who responds with self-justification. Instead will be found a kindly, objective arbiter. It means having one's own inner sense of valuation, rather than looking outside for approval. Instead of falling prey to the cultural collective projections that don't fit, it means knowing who one is and actualizing genuine possibilities. On the cultural level, it means valuing the feminine enough to stand up for it against the collective view of what the feminine is "supposed" to be.

Daughters who have had "too positive" a relation to their father have still another aspect of the father to redeem. If the relation to the father is too positive, the daughters are likely to be bound to the father by over-idealizing him and by allowing their own inner father strength to remain projected outward on the father. Quite often their relationships to men are constricted because no man can match the father. In this

165

case they are bound to the father in a similar way to women who are bound to an imaginary "ghostly lover." (Often an idealized relation to the father is built up unconsciously when the father is missing.) The too positive relationship to the father can cut them off from a real relationship to men and quite often from their own professional potentialities. Because the outer father is seen so idealistically, they can't see the value of their own contribution to the world. To redeem the father in themselves, they need to acknowledge his negative side. They need to experience their father as human and not as an idealized figure in order to internalize the father principle in themselves.

In many ways I see the "Beauty and the Beast" fairy tale as telling the story of this kind of redemption. Beauty loved her father so much! Yet in asking for such a simple gift, a rose, which the father had to steal from the Beast's garden, Beauty had to go and live with the Beast in order to save her father's life. And this was terribly frightening for her. But when she learned to value and love the Beast, he was transformed into his original potentiality as Prince, and the father's life was saved.

Ultimately, redeeming the father entails reshaping the masculine within, fathering that side of oneself. Instead of the "perverted old man" and the "angry, rebellious boy," women need to find "the man with heart", the inner man with a good relation to the feminine.

The cultural task of women today involves the same process. The value of the father principle needs to be seen and its limits need to be recognized as well. Part of this task involves sorting out what is essential to the father and what has been imposed artificially by the culture. Most often the father principle has been split into two conflicting opposites—the rigid, old authoritarian ruler and the playful but irresponsible eternal boy. In Western culture the authoritarian side of the father has been consciously valued and accepted, and the playful, boyish side repressed or consciously devalued. Culturally, this has resulted in the kind of situation found in *Iphigenia in Aulis*. The authoritarian power side makes the decisions (Agamemnon) and sacrifices the daughter, but the initiating cause of the sacrifice comes from the jealousy of the boyish brother (Menelaus). These two sides are at odds on the conscious level, but unconsciously, through their possessiveness, they collude in the sacrifice of the daughter, i.e., the young, emerging feminine. Women today need to confront this split in the father principle and contribute to its healing. In this sense, redeeming the father may entail "re-dreaming" the father, i.e., a feminine fantasy about what the father could be and do. My disappointment with Iphigenia was that finally she went willingly to her death. Even though the outer situation of her sacrifice caused by the trap into which her father had fallen seemed inevitable, she could have spoken out of her feminine instinct and wisdom and told her father what could have been possible. And this might have produced a change in masculine consciousness. Women are just beginning to do this today— they are beginning to share their feelings and fantasies and bring them out in public. Women need to tell their stories. They need to tell men what they expect of them. They need to say it out of their gut and not try to justify their feelings on masculine grounds. But they also need to tell about themselves in the spirit of compassion and not out of bitter defeat. Many women remain trapped in the facticity of their lives, not seeing their own possibility. This leads to bitterness and cynicism. Here is where the value of the puella is redeeming, for its deep connection with the realm of possibility and imagination can lead to new ways of seeing and doing things and to a new valuation of the feminine. When this creative vision is combined with the strength and focus of the Amazon woman, a new understanding and feeling for the father may emerge.

Recently, I asked one of my classes to write down their fantasy of a good father. The class consisted mostly of women in their twenties and early thirties, but there were also a few men. Here is their composite fantasy of a father: Father is a man who is strong, stable, dependable, firm, active, adventurous; yet he is warm, loving, compassionate, tender, nurturing, caring, and involved. Their fantasy of the father was as an androgynous person, i.e., someone who has integrated both the masculine and feminine elements in himself.

A major theme that kept recurring was that the father should provide guidance, both in the outer and inner worlds, but without lecturing or demanding. "Guide and teach, not push and preach" was the way they thought the father should help them to form their own limits, principles, and values and to balance discipline and pleasure. Their emphasis was that the father lead by example and *be* a model of adult confidence, honesty, competence, authority, courage, faith, love, compassion, understanding, and generosity in the areas of work, creativity, social, ethical, and love commitment. At the same time, he would clearly own his values as his own, neither imposing them on his daughter nor representing them as "the only right way." As a guide he would provide both nurturance and advice, yet encourage his daughter to be independent and explore things on her own. On the practical level he would encourage and teach financial management and support any aspirations she might have toward professional work. Believing in her strength, beauty, intelligence, and ability, he would be proud of her. But he would not project his own unfulfilled wishes on his daughter and be dependent or overly protective of her. Rather, he would affirm his daughter's unique and individual way of being, respecting and valuing her personhood, yet not expecting responsibilities beyond her years. He would be sensitive and emotionally available when she needed him throughout the course of her development. And with this good timing and intuitive sense of his daughter, he could offer the protection and guidance she needed at the right time. But when she was ready to become an adult, he would also sense this and withdraw from the role of father to mutual friendship with the necessary respect and love. So he would want and be able to learn from her too. Ultimately, the father and daughter would be able to talk and listen to each other, sharing life experiences and learning from one another.

The father's own life, his own enjoyment and satisfaction and creativity, were important for these daughters. They wanted their father to have built for himself a good life which satisfied and challenged him—a life in which he tested himself and emerged calm, ordered, solid, firm, and reliable, yet loving and able to be open about his feelings and able to express his own wants and needs. A desirable father would take care of himself: emotionally, physically, intellectually, creatively, spiritually. And this self-care would be the ground for his care of his daughter. For these daughters it was crucial that the father be able to ask for help when he needed it. It was crucial that he be able to show his own vulnerability, that he be able to express his feelings openly, sincerely, and honestly rather than stewing and brooding on them or exploding with them. It was also crucial that the father be able to receive the daughter's love for him.

Another extremely important aspect was that his primary emotional relationship be with his wife and not the daughter, so the daughter did not have to provide for his emotional needs and could be free to grow on her own. If the father respected his wife as a strong, independent, competent woman partner, and did not treat the wife as a daughter by being authoritarian, or as a mother by being submissive—this would provide the model of a good marital relationship for the daughter and also would model the respect that man and woman can have for each other. Thus, by the way he related to her mother, he would show how a man might be in a relationship with a mature woman.

The bridge to sexual relationship was another exceedingly important area. The father provides a safe and secure relationship to the opposite sex, to men. If, at the appropriate stage, he can appreciate his daughter's difference and her feminine sexuality, even flirt with her in a safe way, then he could help be a bridge to a healthy sexual relationship later on. By being nonpossessive and supporting her efforts in relating to men, he would help facilitate her growth in this area.

A good relation to his own inner child and a sense of humor were also essential qualities these women desired in their fathers—to be able to play and enjoy his daughter's world, but not to remain a child himself. Most important was that the father be there for them when needed, that he provide consistency and a sense of trust, that he be honest, reliable, and keep his word.

While the integration of all these qualities may sound like an overwhelming and superhuman task, at the same time these daughters did not want their fathers to be "perfect." As one person said, "Father should be human and be entitled to all the emotion that every other human has. If he doesn't know something, he should be able to admit that he doesn't know it." After someone else wrote her description, she said, "This is too ideal. It's making me nervous." Someone else said her own development had been impaired by having a "perfect parent," because other men did not equal his level of devotion, so it was hard to find a satisfying relationship with other men. As she put it, "My father is encouraging and believes I can do anything. I am sometimes delusional enough to believe him."

Redeeming the father also requires redeeming the feminine in oneself—really valuing that mode. Part of the wounded father's problem is that he himself is out of relation to the feminine. Either he is cut off and devalues it by going the route of the rigid patriarch, or he may be too much under its power as in the case of the eternal boy who loses his own ability to act and becomes passive. The first ignores the power of the feminine, and the other gives it too much power by putting it on a pedestal and so, paradoxically, devalues its real value too.

If a woman really values herself and acts out of the unique realm of her needs, feelings, and intuitions, creates in a way that is hers, and experiences her own authority, she is then able really to dialogue with the masculine. Neither is she subservient to the masculine, nor does she imitate it. Valuing what is really one's own in the feminine realm is really hard because it means facing the collective as who one is. The puella tends to buy a collective view of the feminine by accepting the projections, being what the other wants. But the armored Amazon, in imitating the masculine, devalues the feminine by implicitly accepting the masculine as superior.

And what is the feminine? In my experience, this is a question that women are now asking. They are searching, talking with each other, trying to articulate their experiences. Many women feel and experience the feminine, but don't have the words to express it since our language and concepts have been based on masculine models. So redeeming the feminine is a challenging quest just now. It is in process. It is happening! As Muriel Rukeyser expressed it in her poem entitled "Kathe Kollwitz":

> What would happen if one woman told
> the truth about her life? The world
> would split open.[4]

CHAPTER TEN

FINDING FEMININE
SPIRIT

And now we who are writing women and strange monsters
Still search our hearts to find the difficult answers,
Still hope that we may learn to lay our hands
More gently and more subtly on the burning sands.
To be through what we make more simply human,
To come to the deep place where poet becomes woman,
Where nothing has to be renounced or given over
In the pure light that shines out from the lover,
In the warm light that brings forth fruit and flower
And that great sanity, that sun, the feminine power.

May Sarton

When I began writing this book, I thought that writing the
chapter on "Redeeming the Father" would heal the deep
wound I had suffered for so many years. I hoped that the pain
would disappear into a memory from the pale past. But this
was not my experience. Instead I felt more pain. The wound
felt deeper. And I was more vulnerable and open to my
feelings of grief and anger. Once more, I was plunged back
into the father-daughter wound.

172

While I was in the midst of this turmoil and writing the envisioned last chapter of my book ("Redeeming the Father"), I had two dreams. The first occurred a day or two before I started that chapter. It was a horrible dream and I woke up crying for hours! My first female analyst, the woman I loved most and who had been a mother and model to me, had died. She had sent a female messenger from Europe to give me three gifts. The major gift was a huge, hand-carved, golden toilet bowl that actually looked more like a chalice. This exquisite gift was to be in my living room. She also gave me several different pictures of myself taken at the time I first went into analysis. The third gift was some newspaper clippings. I sobbed and kept saying it couldn't be true. My analyst couldn't be dead. I wanted to call Switzerland to find out. But the dream kept repeating itself.

After the initial shock of this dream, I realized its inner symbolic meaning. The death of this woman analyst who had been a mother and feminine model for me, left me on my own. But I had her gifts to take with me. The photographs were the reminder of what I looked like when I started the process of analysis. The news clippings were the reports of what had happened. And the beautiful hand-carved golden chalice-like toilet bowl was the greatest gift she could give me, symbolizing the union of "highest and lowest". My analyst, through her acceptance and example, had given me the possibility for bringing out, valuing, and containing the previously rejected parts of myself—my rage and my tears—as well as my repressed longing for the positive spiritual side of my father. The dream showed clearly the importance of this gift for my life; it was to be placed in the central part of my home, the living room, and not to be relegated to a rejected corner of the house. For me, the dream provided an image for forming and containing my feminine spirit.

The second dream occurred on my birthday, a few days after I had completed writing the "Redeeming the Father" chapter. In that dream, I had asked another woman analyst, with whom I was currently in analysis, to trim and shape my hair and give it a permanent for more body and fullness. For

173

me this meant the shaping of my feminine identity and giving it more permanence and substance.

Redeeming the father was not the last step in my process of trying to heal the wound. My dreams were telling me the final secret lay not in the masculine but the feminine. The paradox of redeeming the father was that ultimately I had to give up projecting spirit onto the father and find it within the feminine. To redeem the father meant finding the feminine spirit in myself!

It occurred to me that my model for healing the wound had been in part a masculine model: the linear notion that progress goes steadily along a straight, hard line to an end point. Whereas my own experience had always been that the path of transformation was more like a circular spiral. Inevitably I came back repeatedly to the central injuries and conflicts, and each time the experience seemed even more painful than the last. The difference was that the period of pain tended to be shorter, that ultimately I had more strength, courage, and ability to deal with these painful issues.

The value of such suffering is expressed in Robert Bly's poem, "What is Sorrow For?".

> What is sorrow for? It is a storehouse
> of wheat, barley, corn, and tears.
> One steps to the door on a round stone.
> The storehouse feeds all the birds of sorrow.
> And I say to myself: Will you have
> sorrow at last? Go on, be cheerful in autumn,
> be stoic, yes, be tranquil, calm,
> or in the valley of sorrows spread your wings.[1]

My sorrow was indeed a storehouse for, after each relapse, the quality of my experience was deeper, more receptive, spontaneous, and joyful. The quality of my life felt more harmonious each time I went around the circle. The image of Psyche's third task, drawing water from the stream that flowed between the highest mountaintop and the depths of the underworld, now was a living image for me. As the philosopher Heidegger, who had been my spiritual father, expressed it: the image of human existence is circular. We live our practical lives in clock-time, he said. Yet we all know that lived time is not primarily linear. An hour spent in an exciting symphony or love or play or anything in which we are deeply involved can be experienced as an intense moment, whereas five minutes of a boring lecture or any other unrelated activity can seem interminable. Time is like an ever-moving spiral, he suggests. The future continually comes toward us but it meets us with our past at each moment of the immediate present. Each time this process happens, we are confronted with mysterious new levels of our being. We must meet the unknown future by bringing to bear everything that has been shaped in us by the past.

This image of the healing process occurring in cyclic time released me from my ego expectation that if I followed steps A, B, C, etc., I would be through with my problems forever. It enabled a rounder, softer vision of myself and my course through life. I also remembered that once I had asked the *I Ching* for an image of transformation of the father-daughter wound. The hexagram I received was "Revolution" (#49), with the second line moving to hexagram #18, "Work on What Has Been Spoiled." This latter hexagram speaks of the original spoiling of the parental image. This was the work to be done.

The hexagram "Revolution" refers specifically to the seasons of transformation. The image is to set the calendar in order and to make the seasons clear. "Man masters these changes in nature by noting their regularity and marking off the passage of time accordingly,"[2] hence adapting appropriately to each season. Following Nature's seasonal cycle is the image I received to illuminate the transformation of the father-daughter wound and for finding feminine spirit.

Inwardly, this means we must accept each season in its turn. As I write now, it is fall—the moment when we enjoy the last glow of ripeness in the golden hours of Indian summer. But we feel also the foreshadowing of the cold time

175

to come, of death and limitation, the hint of the new descent into the dark which must precede the joyous rebirth. Soon it will be winter, the time for accepting the cold outside and going inside, the hibernation and patient waiting which cannot talk of victory but which can hold through and endure the dark. Sometimes the stir of life is felt but one never knows if the birth will succeed. In winter one has to accept that "not knowing" and affirm life without results, affirm life in and of itself. And then comes spring, when life buds and small green shoots appear. It would seem that this season of possibility would be the easiest to accept, and yet we know that suicide rates are high in spring. If one hasn't related properly to winter, if one has fought it and not really accepted the possibility of both birth and death, or if one has gone into it too deeply, forgetting the passage of the seasons, then one may not be able to accept the new and, fearing change, will cling to depression and the old. Many women waste years of their lives, indulging in depression and despair, never accepting their possibilities, refusing to enter the world, refusing spring. Spring means to care for the new possibilities as they grow, to water and feed them. Finally comes summer—the ripening of all those possibilities, putting them into actuality, standing up for them and enjoying it. This seems to me to be the central challenge for women: to be who they are as a whole, accepting both light and dark and the new cycle of seasons to come. The wound is there and part of our experience. So we have to learn to accept and live with it, and yet relate to the new healing possibilities. This requires an active effort, a willingness to go into our depths and to listen and speak out of our feminine experience.

I was struck in the fairy tale of "The Courageous Girl" at how necessary it was to wear men's clothing in order to get the medicine to heal her father's blindness. Other women heroines, Joan of Arc, for example, have also felt it necessary to wear man's clothing to achieve their goals. Taking on "man's clothing" consciously is different from an Amazon armor. For if the disguise is consciously chosen, it can be taken off consciously as well. Sometimes it is necessary to adopt man's clothing to save oneself if one wants to go out into the world and affirm women's values. I think of Rosalind, the heroine of Shakespeare's *As You Like It*. She had to disguise herself to save her life from the evil designs of the duke who had expelled her father. And she chose to stay in that disguise to see how true was the love of Orlando, rather than trying to seduce him through accepting his feminine projections. If a woman is disguised as a man, she can see how her potential lover behaves toward her as a friend. She can also see how her work is regarded by the culture when there are no collective projections applied to it. As Rosalind says when she prepares to take on the man's clothing,

> Alas, what danger will it be to us,
> Maids as we are, to travel forth so far!
> Beauty provoketh thieves sooner than gold.
>
> ...Were it not better,
> Because that I am more than common tall,
> That I did suit me all points like a man?
> A gallant curtlease upon my thigh,
> A boar-spear in my hand, and in my heart
> Lie there what hidden woman's fear there will.
> We'll have a swashing and a martial outside,
> As many other mannish cowards have
> That do outface it with their semblances.[3]

While I see this as a necessary step in the liberation of women, I feel now the time has come for women to wear their own clothing and to speak out of their feminine wisdom and strength. The feminine—what is it? I don't think we can define it. But we can experience it and out of that experience try to express it via symbols and images, art forms through which we can be in the mystery of that experience and yet somehow articulate it too. Recently one woman told me she had, for the first time in her life, experienced what the feminine is. But she couldn't articulate the experience. No words and images had come to her yet. Still that didn't

177

negate the value, intensity, and awareness of that experience. One of the challenges women have today is not only to be open to the experience of the feminine but also to try to express it in their own way.

Recently I asked one of my classes to describe their images and experience of feminine spirit. This same class had described their fantasy of the good father earlier in the term. That was not difficult for them to do and their descriptions of the good father were amazingly similar. But when it came to describing feminine spirit, they were at first stymied. The descriptions were quite different. The one common experience was that none of these women felt they could use their mother as a model. They had to turn to themselves and try to bring out their own experience.

Women are beginning to realize that men have been defining femininity—through their conscious expectations of what women can and cannot do and through their unconscious projections on women. This has resulted in a distorted view not only of women but of the man's inner feminine side as well. Women first need to become conscious of these definitions and projections and say which describe them and which do not. Men can help in this process too. For if they are sensitive to the feminine, receptive and listening, they can add their own experience of femininity to our understanding of it. The poet Rilke was very sensitive to the feminine realm and saw long ago many of the special strengths and unique qualities of feminine spirit. But ultimately women have to tell their own stories out of their own personal experience and feeling, but with an eye to the universal as well.

When women begin to feel confident and to express the values of their own way of being, then they will enable the healing of the masculine. The masculine in women, in men themselves, and in the culture is wounded due to its poor relationship to the feminine. Consider the following dream of a woman whose relation to the father had been wounded.

I am a nurse in a hospital. The patient is an attractive man who is in bed. He has no left arm. Rather than being disabled,

178

there is a feeling of magic about the absence of the arm. With his direction I attach an arm to him. The only feeling is one of love. When I woke up I had a feeling of completion.

This dream shows the woman dreamer her own power to heal the masculine within. She had a wounded relation to the father which had affected her relation to the masculine, but despite that, she had within herself the power to heal this wound. In this case the healing occurs through the joint effort of the man and herself.

Another dream of a man shows the power of the feminine to heal the wounded masculine in individual men and in our culture as well. The dreamer was a warm and related feeling man who valued the feminine in women and in himself to a high degree. The dream reveals the wound in the masculine at an archetypal level and its effect on the culture.

I was going to the house of an unknown dark-haired woman. I lusted after her and had only sex on my mind. When she opened the door I immediately knew she was unusual and that I had something to learn from her. But I still asked about having sex, and she looked at me as if to say "Okay, if that's all you know about." Then the scene changed and I was at President Kennedy's funeral. His body was in the coffin and the hands, arms, legs, and feet were dismembered. Suddenly the dark-haired woman came forward and put the pieces of his body back together, healing him.

This dream reveals the wound in the masculine. The healing power of the feminine symbolized by the unknown, dark-haired woman is present, but at first the dreamer does not acknowledge it and relates to her via the old masculine way of sexual possession. Even so, he knows at a deeper level that she has something to offer him. The redemptive power of feminine healing is dramatically revealed at the end of the dream when the unknown woman puts back together the dismembered body of the president, the cultural ruler of the country.

Here one is reminded of the acknowledgment of this power of feminine healing in ancient mythology. There, the goddess

Isis, Queen of Egypt, found the dismembered bodily parts of King Osiris, her husband, and put them back together, healing him. One part was missing, the phallus. But Isis fashioned a new phallus of wood and attached it to Osiris' body. Here I see a parallel with the tale of "The Handless Maiden." Just as her arms were cut off and a man gave her artificial silver arms until her own regenerated naturally through her ability to accept sorrow, so the creative phallus of Osiris needed the help of a woman for regeneration. In our age of technology, with its emphasis on achievement and control, it is as though the creative phallus has been lost and men have sacrificed their inner daughters to the devil through possessiveness. Frequently they are afraid to acknowledge their wounds and have lost access to their tears. Feminine spirit which has the courage to face both the wound and the power of rage and tears can heal through appreciation of the natural cyclic power of seasonal growth and the earth's ability to receive new seeds of creativity.

NOTES

NOTES FOR CHAPTER ONE

1. For a description of the symbolic view of the feminine as contrasted to the biological and cultural approaches, see Ann Ulanov, *The Feminine in Jungian Psychology and in Christian Theology* (Evanston: Northwestern University Press, 1971), p. 137ff.

2. Jung's view is to see the father symbolically as an archetypal image. One way the father archetype functions is as an image of the patriarchal culture in which women in the West must live. Similarly the daughter archetype can function as a cultural image of the feminine and is subordinate in a patriarchal culture. If there is so much wounding among personal fathers and daughters in our culture, this reflects a problem between the dominant father principle and the subordination of the feminine daughter principle in our culture as a whole. The cultural manifestation of the relationship between the father and daughter principles may be a distortion of their inherent relationship.

3. Vera Von der Heydt has described, from a Jungian viewpoint, the role of the father and the way he functions vis-à-vis his children in her article, "On the Father in Psychotherapy" in *Fathers and Mothers* (Zurich: Spring Publications, 1973), p. 133ff. From another viewpoint the developmental process whereby the father traditionally projects ideals for the daughter is described by H. Kohut, *The Analysis of the Self* (New York: International University Press, 1971), p. 66.

4. The "puer aeternus," or eternal boy, is a phrase Jung borrowed from Ovid, who had used it to name a mischievous, seductive young

181

god. Marie Louise von Franz has described this pattern in her book *Puer Aeternus* (Zurich: Spring Publications, 1970).

5. M. Esther Harding has described the "ghostly lover" in her book, *The Way of All Women* (New York: Harper and Row, 1970), pp. 36-68.

6. Anaïs Nin, *The Diary of Anaïs Nin*, vol. I (New York: Harcourt, Brace and World, Inc.), p. 194.

7. James Hillman has described these two extremes, and their secret interaction, in his article, "Senex and Puer: An Aspect of the Historical and Psychological Present," *Eranos Jahrbuch XXXVI*, 1967.

8. The mother's role in feminine development is an enormous subject and has been written on extensively. For example, Nancy Friday in *My Mother, My Self* (New York: Dell Publishing Co., 1977) explores the effect the mother has on the daughter's search for identity. From a Jungian view point, Erich Neumann analyzes the "The Great Mother" archetype and its relation to the development of consciousness in *The Great Mother* (Princeton: Princeton U. Press, 1963).

9. "Puella" is the Latin word for girl. The "puella aeterna" (eternal girl) is a feminine mode parallel to the masculine "puer aeternus."

10. Søren Kierkegaard, *Fear and Trembling* and *The Sickness Unto Death*, trans. Walter Lowrie (New York: Doubleday and Co., Inc., 1954).

NOTES FOR CHAPTER TWO

1. For a more detailed discussion, see Ulanov, *The Feminine*.

2. Euripides, *"Iphigenia in Aulis"* in *Orestes and Other Plays* (Baltimore: Penguin Books, Inc., 1972) p. 419.

3. Ibid.

4. In some versions, Iphigenia is reported to be saved at the last moment by Artemis, serving as a priestess to this Amazon-like goddess, foreshadowing a compensation which is prevalent in our society today.

5. Ibid., p. 412.

6. Ibid., p. 383.

7. Ibid., p. 411.

8. Ibid., p. 422.

9. Ibid.

10. See Euripides' play, *Electra*.

11. R. Wilhelm, tr., *I Ching: The Book of Changes* (New York: Bollingen Foundation, Inc., 1967), pp. 52-53.

12. Larousse, *World Mythology* (New York: Hamlyn Publishing Group, Limited, 1973), pp. 125-127. This suggests an opposition between lunar Artemis personifying the power of feminine spirit over the masculine wind spirit.

13. Esther Harding has explored the virgin image in relation to the ancient goddesses and has pointed out that symbolically every woman needs to feel and act upon the power and strength of her own unique feminine wisdom, rather than projecting this power upon men. See *Women's Mysteries* (New York: Harper & Row, Publishers, 1976), pp. 103-104, 125.

14. Robert Bly, *News of the Universe* (San Francisco: Sierra Club Books, 1980), p. 256.

15. Ibid., p. 277.

NOTES FOR CHAPTER THREE

1. Henrik Ibsen, *A Doll's House*, trans. R. Sharp and E. Marx-Aveling (New York: Dutton, 1975), pp. 64-65.

2. Ibid., pp. 62-63.

3. Ibid., pp. 66-67.

4. Tennessee Williams, *The Glass Menagerie* (New York: New Directions Books, 1970), p. 23.

5. Anaïs Nin, *A Spy in the House of Love* (Chicago: The Swallow Press, 1959), p. 91.

6. Ibid., p. 109.

7. Arthur Miller, *After the Fall* (New York: The Viking Press, 1968), p. 77.

8. Ibid., pp. 106-107.

9. Kierkegaard, *Sickness Unto Death*, p. 169.

10. Grimm Brothers, *The Complete Grimm's Fairy Tales* (New York: Pantheon Books, 1972), pp. 264-267.

NOTES FOR CHAPTER FOUR

1. June Singer, *Androgyny* (New York: Anchor Books, 1977), p. 61.

2. Rainer Maria Rilke, *Letters to a Young Poet*, trans. M.D. Herter Norton (New York: W.W. Norton and Co., 1963), pp. 58-59.

3. My focus here differs from Toni Wolff's description of the "Amazon" as a type. See Ulanov's discussion of this in *The Feminine* pp. 205-207.

4. Sylvia Plath, *The Bell Jar* (New York: Bantam Books, 1972), p. 2.

5. Ibid., p. 48.

6. Ibid., p. 88.

7. Ibid., p. 193.

8. Ingmar Bergman, *Face to Face*, trans. A. Blair (New York: Pantheon Books, 1976), p. 115.

9. Federico Fellini, *Juliet of the Spirits*, trans. H. Greenfeld (New York: Ballantine Books, 1966), p. 62. Fellini goes on to contrast genuine feminine independence with the masculinization of the woman. He says, "The masculinization of the woman is one of the most horrible things possible. No, woman mustn't emancipate herself for imitation—which would be a development within the projection of that famous masculine shadow—but to discover her own reality, a different one. Different, it seems to me, from that of the man, but profoundly complimentary and integral to it. It would be a step toward a happier humanity." (p. 62).

10. C.G. Jung, *The Collected Works*, vol. 2, trans. R.F.C. Hull (Princeton: Princeton University Press, 1973), pp. 469ff.

11. Alexander Lowen, *Love and Orgasm* (New York: New American Library, 1965), p. 285.

12. C.S. Lewis, *Till We Have Faces* (Grand Rapids: Wm. B. Eerdman's Publishing Co., 1956), pp. 80-81.

13. Ibid., p. 184.

14. Kierkegaard, *Sickness Unto Death*, p. 166.

15. Ibid., p. 200.

16. Wilhelm, tr., *I Ching*, p. 147.

17. Ibid., p. 148.

NOTES FOR CHAPTER FIVE

1. Evelyn J. Hinz., ed., *A Woman Speaks: The Lectures, Seminars and Interviews of Anaïs Nin* (Chicago: The Swallow Press, 1975), pp. 82-83.

2. Bernardo Bertolucci, *Last Tango in Paris* (New York: Dell Publishing Co., 1973), p. 197.

3. Lowen, *Love and Orgasm*, pp. 266-271.

4. Andrew Lang, ed., *The Blue Fairy Book* (New York: Dover Publications, Inc., 1965), pp. 30-50.

5. Bankier, Cosman, Earnshaw, Keefe, Lashgari, Weaver, eds., *The Other Voice* (New York: W.W. Norton Co., Inc., 1976), p. 38.

6. Carlos Casteneda discusses the warrior theme in many of his books. See, for example, *Tales of Power* (New York: Simon and Schuster, 1974).

7. Rilke, *Letters to a Young Poet*, p. 69.

8. Grimm Brothers, *The Complete Grimms' Fairy Tales*, pp., 322-325.

9. Peter Beilensen, trans., *Lotus Blossoms* (New York: The Peter Pauper Press, Inc., 1970), p. 13.

NOTES FOR CHAPTER SIX

1. Robert Bly has discussed Kali's power in many of his workshops. Ann Ulanov has developed this idea from another perspective in her lectures on "the witch".

2. See C.G. Jung's *Answer to Job* (New York: Meridian Books, 1965).

3. Grimm Brothers, *The Complete Grimm's Fairy Tales*, pp. 17-20.

4. Rainer Maria Rilke, *Requiem, and other Poems*, trans. J.B. Leishman (London: The Hogarth Press, 1957), p. 140.

5. Erich Neumann, *Amor and Psyche* (Princeton, N.J.: Princeton University Press, 1971), pp. 43-44.

6. Dawn Brett, "Apotheosis" (unpublished poem).

NOTES FOR CHAPTER SEVEN

1. Rainer Maria Rilke, *Duino Elegies*, trans. J.B. Leishman and Stephen Spender (New York: W.W. Norton & Co., Inc., 1963), p. 21.

2. Ibid., p. 85.

3. Grimm Brothers, *The Complete Grimm's Fairy Tales*, pp. 160-165.

4. Neumann, *Psyche and Amor*, p. 123.

NOTES FOR CHAPTER NINE

1. "The Courageous Girl" in *The Sandalwood Box: Folktales from Tadzhikistan.* (New York: Charles Scribner's Sons), pp. 16-25.

2. Robert Anderson, *I Never Sang for My Father* in *The Best Plays of 1967-1968* (New York: Dodd, Mead and Co., 1968), p. 281.

3. H. Kohut, *Analysis of the Self* (New York: International University Press, 1971), p. 66.

4. Howe and Bass, eds., *No More Masks* (New York: Doubleday-Anchor Books, 1973), p. 103.

NOTES FOR CHAPTER TEN

1. Robert Bly, "What is Sorrow For?" (unpublished poem).

2. Wilhem, tr., *I Ching*, p. 190.

3. *As You Like It*, act 1, sc. 3.

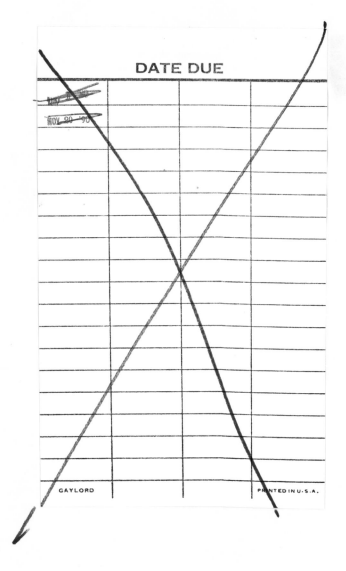